THE KOI FI

A Comprehensive Guide for All Koi Fish Enthusiast,
Covering the Origin of Koi, Pond Setup and Design,
steps for Selecting Healthy Koi, Water Management,
Breeding, And Feeding.

Mark J. Williams

CHAPTER ONE

INTRODUCTION TO KOI FISH

1.1 The History and Origins of Koi

1.1.1 The Journey of Koi from Carp to Ornamental Fish

The history of koi begins with the common carp (Cyprinus carpio), a species native to Eastern Europe and Asia. These carp were initially bred for food over 2,000 years ago in China, where aquaculture practices were essential for sustaining large populations. The carp were hardy and adaptable, making them a staple food source in many regions. However, the transition from utilitarian food fish to ornamental beauty began when these carp were introduced to Japan during the Yayoi Period (300 BCE to 300 CE).

It was in Japan, during the early 19th century, that a significant transformation occurred. In the mountainous regions of Niigata Prefecture, farmers began selectively breeding carp for their unique color mutations. These mutations, initially seen as oddities, piqued the interest of breeders who began refining and enhancing them. Over time, what started as a few colored carp became the foundation for the koi we know today. These fish, referred to as "nishikigoi" in Japan, meaning "brocaded carp," evolved from humble beginnings into vibrant and striking ornamental fish. Varieties such as Kohaku (white with red markings), Taisho Sanke (white with red and black), and Showa (black with red and white) were developed during this period. The selective breeding process was meticulous, with farmers often working for generations to stabilize certain traits like color, pattern, and scale type. The creation of ornamental koi became an art form, and breeding techniques were closely guarded secrets passed down within families.

1.1.2 Koi in Japanese Culture and Symbolism

Koi hold profound significance in Japanese culture, where they have become powerful symbols of perseverance, strength, and good fortune. This symbolism can be traced back to an ancient Chinese legend known as "The Dragon Gate." According to the myth, koi fish would swim upstream through rivers and waterfalls, overcoming tremendous challenges. Those that succeeded in swimming through the Dragon Gate were transformed into dragons, symbolizing transformation through effort and determination. This tale became a metaphor for overcoming life's obstacles and achieving success.

During the Edo Period (1603–1868), koi fish further cemented their place in Japanese culture. Samurai warriors identified with the koi's strength and perseverance, as they saw it as a reflection of their own code of honor and determination. Koi were also thought to bring good fortune and prosperity, making them popular symbols in art, tattoos, and festivals. Even today, koi flags (koinobori) are flown during Japan's Children's Day (Kodomo no Hi) to celebrate the health and strength of children, a tradition that underscores the enduring cultural significance of these fish. In the 20th century, koi breeding became more refined, and koi exhibitions began drawing national attention. New varieties were introduced, and koi became a status symbol in Japanese society. The color and quality of a koi pond were often seen as a reflection of wealth and taste, further solidifying their role as ornamental treasures rather than mere food fish.

1.1.3 Globalization of Koi Keeping

By the mid-20th century, koi keeping had spread beyond Japan, gaining popularity in Europe, North America, and other parts of the world. This global interest was largely driven by the beauty of the fish and the tranquility that koi ponds brought to gardens. In the 1960s and 1970s, koi exhibitions started being held internationally, where breeders from Japan showcased their best fish, further popularizing koi outside Japan. The rise of koi as luxury pets grew rapidly in the late 20th century, particularly in Western countries. Koi became symbols of elegance and refinement, often featured in landscaped ponds in homes and botanical gardens. Collectors and enthusiasts began importing high-quality koi from Japan, and koi farms started to emerge in the U.S., Europe, and other regions to meet growing demand.

International koi competitions also emerged, attracting breeders, collectors, and hobbyists from around the globe. These competitions, often judged based on color, pattern, body shape, and overall health, set the standard for what constituted a "perfect" koi. The All Japan Koi Show, considered the pinnacle of koi competitions, further established koi as an object of admiration and prestige, with some koi fetching prices in the tens of thousands, and even millions, of dollars.

Today, koi keeping has evolved into a global phenomenon. High-end koi are now viewed as living works of art, and koi ponds have become a centerpiece of many homes, estates, and public spaces worldwide. The development of specialized koi food, pond filtration systems, and koi clubs has made caring for koi more accessible, even for beginners.

1.2 Understanding Different Koi Varieties and Color Patterns

Koi are prized for their stunning colors, intricate patterns, and graceful movements in the water. With a wide array of varieties available, each type of koi offers its own unique aesthetic and appeal. Koi fish are generally classified based on their color patterns, markings, and scalation (scale type), and understanding these differences is key to appreciating their beauty.

1.2.1 Basic Overview of Koi Types

The different types of koi are categorized by their specific color combinations, patterns, and scale types. Below are some of the fundamental types of koi that have become the cornerstone of koi appreciation:

- **Kohaku:** This is the most recognized and classic variety, featuring a bright white body (called shiroji) with striking red (known as hi) markings. Kohaku is often considered the foundation of all other koi varieties, as many other types are descendants of this breed.

- **Taisho Sanke (Sanke):** Often referred to simply as Sanke, this koi has a white body adorned with red and black markings. The red patterns resemble those of a Kohaku, while the black markings (known as sumi) add contrast and complexity to its appearance.

- **Showa Sanshoku (Showa):** Similar to Sanke, Showa features red, white, and black, but with a black base instead of a white one. In Showa koi, the black often forms a more prominent part of the pattern, creating dramatic designs that cover more of the body.

- **Utsurimono (Utsuri):** These koi are primarily black with overlaid colors, such as red (Hi Utsuri), yellow (Ki Utsuri), or white (Shiro Utsuri). The bold contrast between the black and the secondary color creates a striking and eye-catching appearance.

- **Butterfly Koi (Longfin Koi):** Known for their elegant, flowing fins, Butterfly Koi are distinguished by their long, delicate pectoral, dorsal, and tail fins. While not a traditional variety from Japan, Butterfly Koi have gained popularity for their graceful movements and beautiful, ethereal look in ponds.

These categories represent just the tip of the iceberg, as there are many more varieties that have been developed over time through selective breeding.

1.2.2 Popular Koi Varieties and Their Features
Kohaku

Kohaku is the quintessential koi and the first variety most enthusiasts learn to recognize. Its clean white body and vibrant red patches have set the standard for koi appreciation. The red markings, known as hi, should be deep and uniform in color, with clear, defined edges. The placement of the hi on the body is critical to the koi's quality; a well-balanced distribution of red markings across the fish adds to its aesthetic appeal. Kohaku are typically judged on the clarity of their white base and the richness of the red, making them one of the most prized koi in competitions.

Taisho Sanke (Sanke)

The Taisho Sanke, named after the Taisho era in Japan when it was first developed, builds upon the simplicity of the Kohaku by adding black (sumi) markings. These black patterns should be crisp and well-defined, often appearing on the koi's upper body rather than on the head. A quality Sanke will have balanced red and black markings that complement each other, without the black overwhelming the red or white. The key to identifying a high-quality Sanke is the clear, clean lines between the three colors, creating a harmonious overall appearance.

Showa Sanshoku (Showa)

Showa koi are similar in color to Sanke, but with a fundamental difference: they have a black base, with red and white patterns overlaid. In contrast to Sanke, where the black is an accent, Showa koi have more prominent black markings that often extend into the head region. Showa koi are prized for their bold patterns, which are often asymmetrical and dynamic. The combination of white, red, and black on a Showa creates a striking contrast that makes these koi highly sought after. Unlike Sanke, a Showa koi's black can cover larger areas, making it appear more dramatic and intense.

Utsurimono (Utsuri)

Utsuri koi are known for their black base color, overlaid with either red (Hi Utsuri), yellow (Ki Utsuri), or white (Shiro Utsuri). The most popular variety is the Shiro Utsuri, where stark white markings stand out against a deep black background. The sumi in Utsuri koi is often solid and bold, creating strong, well-defined patterns that lend a sense of elegance and power to the fish. In competitions, the quality of Utsuri koi is often judged based on the crispness of the contrast between the black and the secondary color, as well as the balance of the markings.

Butterfly Koi

Butterfly koi, also known as longfin koi, are a more recent addition to the koi world, developed through the crossbreeding of traditional koi with wild Indonesian longfin carp. Their most distinguishing feature is their elongated, flowing fins, which create a stunning effect as they glide through the water. Butterfly koi can come in a variety of color patterns, similar to those of traditional koi varieties like Kohaku, Showa, and Sanke. While Butterfly koi are not typically bred for competitions in Japan, they are highly popular in Western countries for their grace and elegance.

1.2.3 Color Patterns and Scalation

Beyond the basic color combinations, koi also exhibit different patterns and scale types that further differentiate the varieties. Some of the notable color patterns include:

- **Bekko:** Bekko koi have a solid white, red, or yellow base with black markings scattered across the body. The black spots should be well-defined and evenly distributed. A white Bekko, known as Shiro Bekko, is especially popular for its clean, minimalistic look.

- **Shusui:** Shusui is a scaleless (doitsu) variety with striking blue and red markings. A distinctive row of scales runs along the koi's dorsal line, creating a unique texture and appearance. Shusui koi often have blue patterns on their backs, with red coloring along the sides and belly.

- **Asagi:** Asagi are known for their beautiful blue and red coloration, with a network of reticulated scales covering the top of the fish. The red is typically found along the belly, fins, and cheeks, while the back is a soft blue, giving the koi a refined and elegant look. The scales of a high-quality Asagi should be clean and neatly arranged, forming a precise net-like pattern.

When selecting koi, look for clear, vibrant colors, well-defined patterns, and symmetrical markings. High-quality koi have smooth, unblemished skin, with no imperfections in the scales or color patches. Proportion is also crucial; koi with a robust and balanced body shape are more desirable in both breeding and competitions.

Selecting Koi by Personal Preference

For beginners, choosing koi based on personal preference is an enjoyable part of the hobby. There's no need to focus solely on the "best" or most expensive varieties—personal taste should play a key role in your selections. Some people may prefer the bold contrast of a Showa, while others might be drawn to the elegance of a Kohaku. Additionally, koi vary in size, so consider the size of your pond and the koi's potential growth when making your selection.

1.3 Koi Behavior and Temperament

Koi are not only admired for their striking appearance, but also for their fascinating behavior and temperament. These fish are social, intelligent, and interactive creatures that can bring life and harmony to any pond. Understanding koi behavior, their social dynamics, and how they interact with humans is key to providing them with a healthy and enriching environment.

1.3.1 Understanding Koi Social Structure

- Koi are highly social animals that thrive in groups, often forming a loosely organized social structure. In their natural state, koi congregate in schools, as this offers safety and social interaction. In a pond setting, they maintain this behavior, preferring to be in the company of other koi or similar species, such as goldfish or other peaceful pond fish. It's important to keep koi in groups of at least three to five, as isolation can lead to stress and negatively affect their mental and physical health.

- Koi are generally peaceful and non-territorial, making them compatible with other non-aggressive species. They are unlikely to display hostile behaviors like fighting or nipping at other fish, even during feeding times, although larger koi might dominate smaller fish to reach food first. Their easy-going nature makes them ideal companions for a community pond. Goldfish, in particular, share similar water and dietary needs, making them perfect pond-mates for koi. However, because koi can grow quite large (up to 36 inches or more), they may outcompete smaller fish for food if not properly managed.

- Koi also establish a subtle hierarchy in their social groups, with larger and more confident fish often taking the lead. While they don't exhibit overt dominance behaviors like many other fish species, the pecking order becomes apparent in feeding patterns and who swims in prime areas of the pond. Social interaction among koi also includes gentle nudging and swimming in sync, behaviors that indicate a healthy and well-adjusted group.

1.3.2 Koi Intelligence and Interaction with Owners

Koi are surprisingly intelligent fish, known for their ability to recognize their owners and even learn simple tricks. Over time, koi can associate the sight or sound of their keeper with food, often swimming toward the edge of the pond or gathering near the surface when their owner approaches. This ability to recognize patterns and learn from experience makes koi more interactive than many other fish species.

Hand-feeding koi is a popular way to bond with them. With patience, koi can be trained to take food directly from your hand, creating a closer connection between owner and fish. This training process begins by consistently feeding them in the same spot and gradually moving your hand closer to the water's surface. As the koi become more comfortable, they will begin to trust their owner and take food from the hand without hesitation. This not only creates a personal bond but also allows for closer observation of the koi's health and behavior. Beyond hand-feeding, koi can learn to follow their owners' movements, cluster in specific areas when called, and even perform simple tricks like swimming through hoops or responding to feeding bells. Their ability to engage with humans and their environment highlights their intelligence and capacity for learning.

1.3.3 Swimming and Feeding Patterns

Koi are graceful swimmers, gliding through the water in slow, fluid movements. Their swimming behavior is generally calm, reflecting their peaceful nature. They tend to swim in a coordinated, school-like formation when in groups, often moving in sync with one another. This behavior is a sign of a healthy and well-adjusted koi community. Healthy koi swim near the middle to lower regions of the pond, exploring the water column and occasionally coming to the surface.

Feeding time is one of the most exciting periods for koi, as they tend to cluster at the water's surface when food is introduced. Their feeding behavior is deliberate and coordinated, with the larger, more dominant koi typically taking the lead. While koi are omnivorous and will eat both plant matter and small aquatic organisms, in a pond setting, they rely on commercial pellets, vegetables, and treats like worms and shrimp. Koi should be fed small amounts at regular intervals rather than large meals, as this is more reflective of their natural grazing behavior. Koi feeding behavior can reveal a lot about their health and the pond's environment. Koi that eagerly swim to the surface and actively compete for food are generally healthy. However, if a koi shows a lack of appetite or refuses to come to the surface during feeding, it can be a sign of illness or stress. Overfeeding should also be avoided, as koi will eat beyond their needs, leading to water quality issues and obesity. Observing swimming patterns is equally important in monitoring their well-being. Healthy koi will explore the entire pond and swim in smooth, consistent motions. If you notice koi hovering near the surface for extended periods, swimming erratically, or showing signs of lethargy, it may indicate problems such as poor water quality, low oxygen levels, or the presence of parasites.

1.3.4 Signs of Stress or Unusual Behavior

Like any other fish, koi exhibit certain behaviors when they are stressed or unwell, and early identification of these signs is crucial for maintaining their health. Some of the most common signs of stress or illness in koi include:

- **Erratic swimming:** Koi that dart around the pond, swim in spirals, or show a lack of coordination may be experiencing stress or suffering from a parasitic infection. Erratic behavior often signals discomfort, especially when coupled with rubbing against surfaces or jumping out of the water.

- **Isolation from the group:** Koi are naturally social and tend to swim together. A koi that isolates itself from the group, hides in one corner of the pond, or avoids interaction with other fish may be sick or stressed. This could be caused by factors such as bullying, water quality issues, or internal health problems.

- **Hovering near the water's surface:** If koi spend prolonged periods at the surface, particularly gasping for air, it could indicate low oxygen levels in the pond. This is a sign that the water may be too warm, overstocked, or not adequately aerated. In some cases, it may also be a sign of bacterial infections affecting the gills.

- **Lethargy or slow movement:** Healthy koi are typically active, curious, and graceful swimmers. Lethargy, reduced movement, or a koi that spends most of its time at the bottom of the pond without foraging or exploring can be a sign of illness.

Common causes of lethargy include poor water quality, parasites, and bacterial infections.

- **Clamped fins:** When koi hold their fins tightly against their bodies rather than spreading them naturally, it's often a sign of stress or discomfort. Clamped fins are commonly associated with poor water quality, parasitic infections, or exposure to toxins.

- **Changes in color:** Koi may lose some of their vibrant coloration when under stress or ill. A sudden fading of color, blotches, or a dull appearance can indicate a health issue, often related to water quality or infection.

Identifying these signs early allows for quick intervention, whether through water testing, medical treatment, or improving pond conditions. Regular observation of your koi's behavior will help ensure they remain healthy and happy.

CHAPTER TWO

DESIGNING YOUR PERFECT KOI POND

2.1 Factors to Consider Before Building a Koi Pond

Building a koi pond is an exciting project that can enhance the beauty of your outdoor space while providing a healthy environment for your fish. However, it requires careful planning to ensure the pond meets the needs of both the koi and the owner. Here's an in-depth look at the key factors to consider before embarking on your koi pond journey.

2.1.1 Purpose of the Pond

Before diving into the technical aspects of pond building, it's essential to determine the primary purpose of the pond. This will guide every other decision, from size and layout to equipment and features. Here are some common purposes to consider:

- **Decorative Ponds:** If the pond's primary purpose is to serve as a beautiful garden feature, the focus will be on aesthetics. This might include design elements like natural stone borders, water features such as fountains or waterfalls, and the incorporation of aquatic plants. While the koi will still be a significant aspect, the design and placement of the pond will prioritize how it looks in your overall landscape. A decorative pond may also be smaller, with fewer koi to maintain a balance between aesthetics and functionality.

- **Koi Breeding Ponds:** If you're interested in breeding koi, the pond design will need to focus on the koi's reproductive health and safety. Koi breeders require deeper ponds to accommodate the spawning process and protect eggs from predators. Special attention will also need to be given to water quality, filtration systems, and a stable environment to ensure the health of breeding pairs and offspring. Separate sections for fry (baby koi) may be necessary, and plants or spawning mats can be incorporated to encourage successful breeding.

- **Exhibition Ponds:** For those planning to showcase large, prized koi or hold exhibitions, the pond needs to be much larger, with exceptional water clarity and filtration systems that maintain optimal conditions. Exhibition ponds should be designed with clear viewing spaces, perhaps even incorporating glass panels for underwater viewing. Depth, size, and advanced filtration will be critical, as these ponds need to support a higher fish population and provide ample swimming space for large koi. Accessibility for maintenance and the ability to easily transport koi for shows will also be important considerations.

Each of these goals has specific design and care requirements that influence the final layout, equipment, and ongoing maintenance of the pond.

2.1.2 Budget Planning

Building a koi pond can range from a relatively affordable backyard project to a costly endeavor, depending on the pond's size, design, and features. Breaking down the costs involved will help you plan a pond that fits your budget while still meeting your goals. Key costs to consider include:

1. Materials

- **Liner:** Pond liners come in different materials, such as PVC, EPDM (rubber), or concrete. Rubber liners are typically the most durable but also the most expensive, while concrete ponds require more labor and maintenance but provide a permanent, solid structure.

- **Filtration systems:** A quality filtration system is one of the most critical components of a koi pond. Filtration equipment includes mechanical, biological, and chemical filters, and for larger ponds, UV sterilizers to control algae. Advanced systems that ensure crystal-clear water will add to the cost.

- **Pumps and aeration:** Proper water circulation is essential to oxygenate the pond and keep the water clean. The size of your pond will dictate the strength and type of pump required, and in some cases, additional aeration systems like air stones or fountains may be necessary.

2. Equipment

- **Skimmers and bottom drains:** These are necessary to prevent debris build-up and keep the water quality high. Larger ponds often require multiple skimmers and drains.

- **Heating systems:** In colder climates, you may need to invest in pond heaters to keep the water temperature stable during the winter months. This can significantly impact the initial setup cost and ongoing electricity expenses.

- **Labor:** Depending on the complexity of your pond, you may need to hire professionals for excavation, liner installation, and setting up the filtration system. While DIY projects can save on costs, larger or more complex ponds are best handled by experts to ensure the structure's longevity and the koi's well-being.

- **Ongoing maintenance:** Don't forget to account for the cost of maintaining the pond. This includes electricity to run pumps and filters, cleaning supplies, water treatments, fish food, and replacement parts for any equipment. Over time, you may also want to invest in aesthetic upgrades or new koi, all of which should be factored into the long-term budget.

For those on a limited budget, consider starting with a smaller pond, using DIY-friendly materials, or opting for more affordable filtration systems initially, with the possibility of upgrading as your koi grow and your budget allows.

2.1.3 Space and Aesthetic Considerations

The available space in your yard or garden will heavily influence the design and size of your koi pond. Before beginning construction, evaluate the space carefully:

- **Assess available space:** Choose an area where the pond will not overwhelm the garden, but still offers enough room for the koi to thrive. A common guideline is to allow at least 1,000 gallons of water for koi to live healthily, with larger ponds being preferable to accommodate the growth of the fish.

- **Consider sunlight and shade:** Koi ponds should have a balance of sunlight and shade. Too much direct sunlight can overheat the water, encourage excessive algae growth, and stress the koi. Ideally, the pond should receive sunlight for part of the day but also have shaded areas, which can be created using aquatic plants, trees, or artificial covers.

- **Incorporate natural elements:** Many koi pond owners like to enhance the pond with surrounding features such as rocks, plants, and waterfalls. This not only improves the visual appeal of the pond but also creates a more natural environment for the koi. Plants like water lilies and lotus can offer shade and shelter for the fish, while adding rocks or driftwood can give the pond a more organic feel. However, when incorporating plants, be mindful that koi may nibble on them, so choose plant species that are resistant to being uprooted.

- **Aesthetic goals:** Consider how the pond will blend with existing garden features. For example, a formal garden may suit a more structured, geometric pond with clean lines and modern materials, while a natural garden might benefit from a free-form pond surrounded by rocks and plant life. Waterfalls and fountains are popular features that add movement and sound, enhancing the calming atmosphere of a koi pond.

2.1.4 Long-Term Maintenance Commitment

Building the pond is only the beginning—ongoing maintenance is essential to keeping your koi healthy and the pond in top condition. It's important to understand the long-term commitment involved:

- **Water quality monitoring:** Koi are sensitive to changes in water quality. Regular testing for pH levels, ammonia, nitrates, and dissolved oxygen is essential. Installing a high-quality filtration system will help manage waste and debris, but you'll still need to check water conditions frequently.

- **Pond cleaning:** Debris like leaves, algae, and fish waste will accumulate in the pond over time. Regular cleaning is necessary to prevent water quality from deteriorating. This can include using skimmers to remove surface debris, vacuuming the bottom of the pond, and manually removing algae. Periodic deep cleaning may also be required to maintain a healthy environment.

- **Filter maintenance:** Filtration systems need to be cleaned and checked regularly. Biological filters, which support beneficial bacteria, must be maintained to avoid clogs, while mechanical filters may need to be flushed or replaced every few months.

- **Fish health and pond care:** Koi care goes beyond the pond itself. You'll need to feed your fish daily, monitor their health, and occasionally treat them for common diseases or injuries. Keeping a watchful eye on their behavior and overall condition will help you address issues early. Additionally, during the colder months, you may need to take extra steps to protect your koi, such as using pond heaters or ensuring the pond doesn't freeze over.

- **Seasonal maintenance:** Each season brings unique challenges. Spring may require cleaning out debris from winter, while summer may involve managing algae growth and providing shade to prevent overheating. Fall requires removing leaves and preparing for winter, and during winter, you'll need to ensure the pond remains aerated and free from ice blockages.

2.2 Choosing the Right Location

Selecting the ideal location for your koi pond is a crucial decision that will impact not only the health and well-being of your koi but also the overall aesthetic and functionality of your outdoor space. Here's a detailed guide to help you choose the best spot for your pond, considering sunlight, environmental factors, utilities, and safety.

2.2.1 Sunlight and Shade Requirements

The balance between sunlight and shade is essential for maintaining a healthy pond ecosystem. Koi thrive in water temperatures between 59°F and 77°F (15°C to 25°C), and the pond's exposure to sunlight can significantly influence these conditions.

- **The Role of Sunlight:** Sunlight is beneficial for koi ponds in moderation. It promotes plant growth, warms the water, and enhances the pond's visual appeal. Aquatic plants such as water lilies rely on sunlight to thrive, and they provide much-needed shade and shelter for your koi. Ideally, the pond should receive about 4-6 hours of sunlight per day, especially in the morning when the sun is less intense. Morning sun helps to gently warm the pond, making the water comfortable for koi without causing a sharp rise in temperature.

- **Dangers of Excessive Sunlight:** Too much direct sunlight, especially in the afternoon, can lead to rapid algae growth, which not only clouds the water but also competes with koi for oxygen, potentially causing stress. Excessive sunlight can also cause the pond water to overheat, particularly in shallow areas, which can be harmful to the koi. High water temperatures reduce oxygen levels in the pond, making it difficult for the koi to breathe. Moreover, fluctuating temperatures can weaken the koi's immune system, making them more susceptible to diseases.

- **Managing Shade:** On the other hand, too much shade can inhibit plant growth and prevent beneficial plants from thriving. Without enough sunlight, oxygenating plants may struggle to survive, reducing the overall oxygen levels in the pond. Lack of sunlight can also affect the koi's activity levels, as koi are more active in warm, well-lit environments. When positioning your pond, try to ensure it receives partial shade during the hottest part of the day, such as in the afternoon. You can achieve this by placing the pond near taller structures or by planting shrubs and trees a short distance away to provide indirect shade. However, as discussed below, it's essential to avoid placing the pond too close to trees.

- **Tips for Sunlight Positioning:** An ideal location for a koi pond is one that receives morning sunlight and is shaded in the afternoon. If natural shading isn't available, you can install artificial shading solutions, such as pergolas, shade sails, or even floating plants like water lilies, which provide natural shade while enhancing the pond's beauty.

2.2.2 Avoiding Trees and Shrubs

While trees and shrubs can add beauty to the landscape around a koi pond, placing the pond too close to them can create long-term maintenance issues. Here are the reasons to avoid planting too close to trees and shrubs:

- **Falling Leaves and Debris:** One of the main reasons to avoid placing a pond near trees is the constant accumulation of falling leaves and organic debris. As leaves fall into the pond, they sink to the bottom and decompose, contributing to waste build-up and increasing the load on the filtration system. Decomposing organic material can also lead to spikes in harmful chemicals like ammonia and nitrates, which can negatively affect the koi's health. Regular removal of leaves is time-consuming, and if neglected, it can lead to murky water and an unhealthy pond environment.

- **Tree Roots:** Tree roots, especially from larger trees, can pose a significant risk to the structural integrity of the pond over time. As tree roots grow, they may penetrate or shift the pond liner, leading to leaks or damage that can be costly to repair. Additionally, root systems can draw water from the pond, potentially lowering the water level and causing stress to the koi.

- **Overhanging Branches:** Trees with overhanging branches can also block sunlight, preventing the pond from receiving adequate light. As mentioned earlier, this can inhibit plant growth and disrupt the balance of the pond ecosystem.

For these reasons, it's advisable to position your koi pond at least several feet away from trees and large shrubs. If you still want to incorporate trees into your pond's surroundings, consider planting species with shallow, non-invasive roots and minimal leaf drop, or install protective barriers between the tree roots and the pond.

2.2.3 Proximity to Utilities

When planning the location of your koi pond, consider the practical aspects of pond maintenance and equipment installation. A well-placed pond should be close to essential utilities, such as electricity and water.

- **Access to Electrical Outlets:** Koi ponds rely on a variety of equipment, including filtration systems, pumps, UV clarifiers, heaters, and possibly lighting or aerators. These all require electricity, so it's important to place the pond within reach of a reliable power source. Ideally, the pond should be located within 50-100 feet of an outdoor electrical outlet. If no outlet is available, you may need to have one professionally installed to safely run your pond equipment. Remember to use GFCI (Ground Fault Circuit Interrupter) outlets for added safety, particularly near water.

- **Water Supply for Maintenance:** Regular water changes are essential for maintaining water quality in a koi pond, especially if the pond is stocked with several koi. Having easy access to a nearby water supply, such as a garden hose or an outdoor faucet, will make filling and topping off the pond more convenient. Additionally, you'll need a water source for periodic cleaning of filters and other equipment. Positioning the pond near a water source can save time and effort during routine maintenance.

- **Drainage and Runoff Management:** Water management is another important factor when choosing the location for your pond. Heavy rainfall or poor drainage can cause water runoff to flow into the pond, bringing with it dirt, fertilizers, and chemicals from surrounding areas. This can drastically affect the water quality and harm the koi. Be sure to locate the pond in a slightly elevated area or install proper drainage systems to divert rainwater away from the pond. Avoid low-lying areas where water may collect during storms, as this can flood the pond or damage the surrounding landscape.

2.2.4 Visibility and Accessibility

A koi pond is not only a home for your fish but also a central feature in your garden or yard. Therefore, it's important to choose a location that is both visually appealing and accessible for maintenance and enjoyment.

- **Visibility for Enjoyment:** Position the pond in a location that is easily visible from frequently used areas, such as patios, decks, or living room windows. This way, you can enjoy the beauty and calming presence of the pond even from inside the house. If your garden is a space for relaxation or entertaining guests, consider placing the pond in a central area where it can be a focal point of the landscape. Installing lighting around the pond can enhance its visibility and appeal in the evening as well.

- **Accessibility for Maintenance:** While aesthetic considerations are important, it's equally crucial to choose a location that allows easy access for maintenance tasks like cleaning, water changes, and equipment repairs. Make sure there's enough room around the pond for you to move freely when performing these tasks. Consider placing the pond near a pathway or creating a walkway around it to make maintenance more convenient.

- **Safety Considerations:** If you have children or pets, safety should be a top priority when deciding on the location of your koi pond. Choose a spot where you can easily monitor the pond to ensure that children and pets do not accidentally fall in. Installing safety features, such as barriers, fencing, or pond covers, can help prevent accidents. You may also want to avoid placing the pond too close to areas where children play or pets roam freely.

2.3 Pond Size and Depth Requirements

Building a koi pond that meets the specific needs of koi fish is key to creating a healthy, balanced ecosystem where they can thrive. Koi fish have unique requirements related to space, depth, and water quality, which are directly influenced by the size and layout of their pond. Here's a comprehensive guide to understanding the optimal pond size and depth for koi.

2.3.1 Ideal Pond Size for Koi Fish

The size of the pond is one of the most critical factors in koi keeping, as it affects the overall health, growth, and behavior of the fish. Koi are large, active fish that can grow quite rapidly, and they require plenty of space to swim freely. A larger pond not only gives koi more room to grow but also provides several additional benefits:

- **Improved Water Quality:** In a larger pond, water quality tends to be more stable because there is a greater volume of water to dilute waste products like ammonia, nitrites, and nitrates, which can be harmful to koi. This means less frequent water changes and better overall health for the fish. Additionally, a larger body of water is less prone to sudden changes in temperature or pH, both of which can be stressful for koi.

- **Better Filtration and Circulation:** Larger ponds can accommodate more robust filtration systems and allow for better water circulation, which is essential for maintaining oxygen levels and distributing nutrients. Proper filtration helps remove harmful substances and keep the water clean, while good circulation ensures that oxygen is evenly distributed throughout the pond, reducing the risk of "dead zones" where the water becomes stagnant.

- **More Space for Swimming and Socialization:** Koi are social fish that interact with each other, and a larger pond provides them with the necessary space to establish their natural behaviors. Crowding koi in a small pond can lead to stress, which weakens their immune systems and makes them more susceptible to disease. Additionally, koi are active swimmers and need space to move around freely to stay healthy.

- **Minimum Size Recommendations:** For a small koi pond, a minimum size of 1,000 gallons is generally recommended. This size can comfortably house a few juvenile koi, but as the fish grow, more space will be needed. As a rule of thumb, plan for about 250 gallons of water per adult koi. If you plan to keep multiple koi, a pond with at least 3,000 to 5,000 gallons of water will offer a more suitable environment. Larger ponds (5,000 gallons or more) are ideal for koi enthusiasts who want to keep a larger population of koi or encourage breeding.

2.3.2 Depth Considerations

The depth of a koi pond is just as important as the surface area, as it plays a critical role in the pond's temperature regulation, predator protection, and overall water quality. A deeper pond ensures a more stable environment for koi, particularly during seasonal changes.

- **Protection from Predators:** One of the primary reasons for having a deeper pond is to protect koi from predators. Birds like herons and raccoons often target koi ponds, and a shallow pond makes it easier for them to capture the fish. A pond depth of at least 3 to 4 feet (1 to 1.2 meters) allows koi to retreat to the bottom, where predators are less likely to reach them. You can further enhance predator protection by creating steep sides or adding overhanging plants or netting to discourage intruders.

- **Temperature Stability:** Koi are sensitive to temperature fluctuations, and deeper ponds provide better temperature regulation. During hot summers, the water at the surface of a shallow pond can heat up quickly, making the environment uncomfortable or even dangerous for the koi. In deeper ponds, koi can escape to the cooler water near the bottom. Similarly, in winter, deeper ponds are less likely to freeze completely, which is crucial in colder climates. Koi need at least 3-4 feet of depth to survive winter hibernation (torpor) without the risk of freezing solid.

- **Stable Water Conditions:** A deeper pond also promotes more stable water conditions in terms of pH, oxygen levels, and clarity. Algae growth tends to be more prolific in shallow water, especially when exposed to direct sunlight, leading to murky water and higher maintenance demands. A deeper pond reduces the intensity of sunlight penetration, which helps prevent excessive algae blooms and keeps the water clearer.

- **Recommended Depth:** A minimum depth of 3 to 4 feet is recommended for koi ponds, but for larger, more mature koi, a depth of 5 to 6 feet (1.5 to 1.8 meters) is preferable. Deeper ponds create a more stable and comfortable environment, especially in regions with extreme weather conditions. If you live in an area with very cold winters, consider building the pond at least 5 feet deep to ensure the water remains unfrozen in the lower layers, providing a safe space for the koi to overwinter.

2.3.3 Shape and Layout of the Pond

The shape and layout of the koi pond not only affect its aesthetic appeal but also influence water circulation, debris accumulation, and the overall functionality of the pond.

- **Aesthetic Considerations:** Koi ponds come in various shapes, including rectangular, circular, and freeform designs. The shape you choose should complement your landscape and reflect your personal style, but it's also important to consider how the shape will impact water movement and debris management. Freeform ponds, which mimic natural bodies of water, often blend more seamlessly into a garden landscape and can incorporate natural elements like rocks, plants, and waterfalls. Rectangular or circular ponds may offer a more structured and formal appearance, making them ideal for smaller spaces or modern designs.

- **Water Flow and Circulation:** When designing the shape of your pond, consider how the layout will affect water circulation. Koi ponds need good water movement to prevent stagnation, distribute oxygen, and help the filtration system work efficiently. A pond with many corners or dead spots can result in areas of poor circulation, where debris can accumulate and oxygen levels drop. For optimal circulation, avoid overly complex shapes with too many bends or narrow sections. Installing aerators, water features, or strategically placed pumps can help promote consistent water movement throughout the pond.

- **Avoiding Shallow Areas:** Shallow areas in a pond may look visually appealing, especially for showcasing plants, but they can become problematic in koi ponds. Shallow regions can accumulate debris like leaves and dirt, and the water can heat up more quickly, leading to algae growth and poor water quality. It's best to avoid creating large shallow zones, particularly if the pond is located near trees or other sources of debris. If you do incorporate shallow areas for plants, make sure they are easy to access for cleaning and maintenance.

2.3.4 Allowing Space for Future Growth

Koi are known for their impressive growth potential. While juvenile koi may only be a few inches long when you first introduce them to the pond, they can reach lengths of 2 to 3 feet (60 to 90 cm) as they mature. Planning ahead for their growth is essential to avoid overcrowding and ensure your koi have enough space to thrive.

- **Growth Rate and Size:** Koi grow relatively quickly, especially when provided with proper nutrition and a clean environment. On average, koi can grow about 6 inches per year in their early years, and some varieties can reach their full size within a few years. It's important to remember that koi do not stop growing once they reach adulthood—given enough space, they will continue to grow throughout their lives.

- **Swimming Space:** As koi grow, they require more space for swimming and social interaction. Crowding can lead to stress, which weakens the fish's immune system and makes them more susceptible to illness. If you start with a small pond, you may need to expand it or reduce the number of koi as they grow larger. For long-term planning, aim to provide at least 250 gallons of water per adult koi, and consider a larger pond if you plan to keep a collection of multiple koi varieties.

- **Planning for Future Additions:** Many koi enthusiasts find themselves adding more fish to their ponds over time, as koi breeding and raising can become a rewarding hobby. If you anticipate expanding your collection, it's wise to build a larger pond from the start to accommodate future additions without compromising water quality or space.

2.4 Pond Liner and Construction Materials

Selecting the right materials for building your koi pond is crucial for its longevity, durability, and functionality. The pond liner, construction materials, and edging not only affect the pond's aesthetic appeal but also play a significant role in maintaining water quality and preventing leaks. Here's an in-depth guide to choosing the right pond liner and construction materials.

The pond liner serves as the waterproof barrier that holds the water in the pond, making it one of the most important decisions when constructing a koi pond. Various types of pond liners are available, each with its advantages and drawbacks, depending on your pond's size, shape, and long-term goals.

2.4.1 EPDM Rubber Liners

EPDM (Ethylene Propylene Diene Monomer) rubber liners are among the most popular choices for koi ponds, and for good reason. They offer a number of benefits that make them ideal for large or irregularly shaped ponds.

- **Durability and Flexibility:** EPDM liners are incredibly durable, often lasting 20 to 30 years or more with proper care. Their flexibility allows them to conform easily to irregularly shaped ponds, making them perfect for custom designs. The material can stretch without tearing, even when placed over rocks or other uneven surfaces.

- **UV and Temperature Resistance:** One of the standout features of EPDM liners is their resistance to UV rays and temperature fluctuations. This ensures that the liner doesn't degrade easily when exposed to sunlight or extreme weather conditions, which is particularly important for ponds in sunny or harsh climates.

- **Environmental Safety:** EPDM rubber is fish-safe, meaning it doesn't leach harmful chemicals into the water. This is crucial for maintaining a healthy ecosystem for your koi and other aquatic life.

- **Installation:** While EPDM liners are highly flexible, they require careful handling during installation to avoid creasing or creating folds that might trap debris. The material is also relatively heavy, so enlisting help for larger installations may be necessary.

2.4.2 PVC Liners

PVC (Polyvinyl Chloride) liners are a more affordable option compared to EPDM, making them attractive for smaller or budget-conscious pond projects.

- **Affordability:** PVC liners are typically less expensive than EPDM, which makes them a viable option for hobbyists looking to build a small pond. However, while cost-effective upfront, they may not offer the same long-term durability as EPDM.

- **Flexibility and Shape Adaptability:** Like EPDM, PVC is flexible and can be molded to fit various pond shapes. However, it is generally less durable and more prone to damage from sharp objects or heavy loads. Over time, PVC liners can become brittle when exposed to direct sunlight and temperature changes, leading to cracks or leaks.

- **Lifespan:** PVC liners have a shorter lifespan than EPDM, typically lasting 5 to 10 years before they need to be replaced. For koi ponds intended to last for decades, this can be a drawback, as maintenance and replacement of the liner can be time-consuming and costly.

- **UV Resistance:** Some higher-quality PVC liners come with UV inhibitors to slow down degradation from sun exposure, but this feature may not be present in all products. If opting for a PVC liner, choose one specifically designed for outdoor ponds.

2.4.3 Preformed Pond Liners

Preformed pond liners are rigid, molded liners that are pre-shaped into specific designs, making them easy to install.

- **Ease of Installation:** Preformed liners are a great choice for beginners because they are straightforward to install. Unlike flexible liners that require careful shaping and folding, preformed liners simply need to be placed into the ground and leveled.

- **Limited Design Flexibility:** The main disadvantage of preformed liners is their lack of design flexibility. Since they come in pre-set shapes and sizes, you are limited to the manufacturer's available designs. This can make it harder to customize your pond to fit a specific landscape or aesthetic preference.

- **Durability:** Preformed liners are usually made of hard plastic or fiberglass, which makes them durable against punctures and tears. However, they are more prone to cracking if the ground shifts or the liner is not properly supported during installation.

2.4.4 Concrete Ponds

For those seeking a permanent, large-scale koi pond, concrete is the most durable option, though it requires professional installation and comes with additional considerations.

- **Permanent and Customizable:** Concrete ponds offer unparalleled durability and customization. Because concrete can be shaped and molded to any form, it's ideal for those who want complete control over the pond's design, including complex features like waterfalls or integrated shelves.

- **Durability:** Once cured and sealed properly, a concrete pond can last for decades without needing replacement, making it a great choice for those who want a long-lasting pond. It is also highly resistant to damage from sharp objects, unlike flexible liners.

- **Professional Installation:** Installing a concrete pond is not a DIY-friendly project. It requires specialized skills to ensure the structure is waterproof and resistant to cracking. Proper sealing is essential; as even minor cracks can lead to leaks over time. If not sealed properly, concrete can also alter the water's pH levels, which can be harmful to koi.

- **Cost:** Concrete ponds are among the most expensive options due to the material and labor involved. However, for those looking to build a large, permanent pond, the investment can be worthwhile for the durability and customizability offered.

2.4.5 Adding Underlayment

Underneath any pond liner, it's important to add an underlayment to protect the liner from punctures or damage caused by sharp objects such as rocks or roots. Skipping this step can result in costly repairs or the need to replace the liner entirely. Several materials can be used for underlayment:

- **Geotextile Fabric:** This is the most common underlayment material, made of a thick, nonwoven fabric that acts as a cushion beneath the liner. It's durable, flexible, and easy to install, providing protection against sharp objects.

- **Sand:** Some pond builders use a layer of sand as an additional protective measure beneath the liner. Sand can smooth out uneven ground, but it should be used in combination with a geotextile underlayment for maximum protection.

- **Old Carpet or Carpet Padding:** For budget-conscious projects, old carpet or carpet padding can be repurposed as an underlayment material. While not as durable as geotextile fabric, it still provides some protection against punctures.

2.4.6 Pond Edging Materials

The edging of your pond serves both an aesthetic and practical purpose. It frames the pond, helping to integrate it into the landscape, and prevents erosion and debris from entering the water.

Natural Stone

Natural stone is a popular choice for pond edging due to its beauty and durability. Stones like slate, granite, and flagstone create a natural, rustic look that complements the pond environment.

- **Durability and Weight:** Natural stones are heavy and durable, making them effective at holding the pond liner in place and preventing erosion. Their weight also discourages animals or pets from disturbing the pond edges.

- **Integration with Landscape:** Stones can be arranged to create a seamless transition between the pond and surrounding landscape. You can use a variety of sizes and shapes to create a layered or tiered effect around the pond, adding depth and texture.

Bricks and Pavers

For a more formal or structured look, bricks and pavers are a great option for pond edging.

- **Clean, Structured Look:** Bricks and pavers offer a clean, geometric look that works well in formal garden designs. They are available in a variety of colors and patterns, allowing you to match the pond edging with your home's architecture or landscape design.

- **Ease of Installation:** Pavers and bricks are relatively easy to install, and they provide a sturdy, stable edge that helps prevent soil erosion.

Pond Coping

Pond coping stones are specifically designed for use along the edges of ponds. They provide a finished, polished look while also serving the practical function of holding the liner in place.

- **Blending with the Environment:** Coping stones come in various natural finishes and colors, allowing them to blend seamlessly with your pond's design. They provide a smooth, stable edge for the pond, which can be beneficial if you plan to install a pond cover or netting.

Preventing Erosion and Runoff

No matter what material you use for the pond edge, it's important to consider how water runoff will be managed. Without proper edging, soil and debris can easily wash into the pond, causing murky water and requiring more frequent cleaning. Ensure the pond edge is slightly elevated above the surrounding landscape to direct runoff away from the pond. Use plants, rocks, or mulch to stabilize the edges and reduce soil erosion.

2.5 Essential Pond Equipment: Filters, Pumps, and Aeration Systems

To maintain a healthy environment for your koi, installing the right equipment is essential for optimal water quality and circulation. The proper filtration, pumping, and aeration systems help to create a balanced ecosystem, ensuring that the pond is clean, oxygenated, and suitable for koi. Here's a detailed guide on the essential equipment for koi ponds and how each component contributes to a thriving aquatic habitat.

2.5.1 Importance of Filtration Systems

A koi pond requires efficient filtration to keep the water clean, clear, and free of harmful waste products. Filtration systems perform two critical functions:

- **Mechanical Filtration:** Removes physical debris such as uneaten food, leaves, and fish waste from the water. This prevents the accumulation of organic matter that can cloud the water and clog other equipment.

- **Biological Filtration:** Breaks down harmful chemicals like ammonia and nitrites, produced by fish waste, into less toxic compounds. This biological process is essential for maintaining a stable, healthy environment for koi.

A proper filtration system combines these two processes, ensuring that both large debris and invisible toxins are addressed.

Mechanical Filtration

Mechanical filtration is the first line of defense in keeping your pond water clean. This type of filtration works by physically trapping and removing particles from the water before they have a chance to decompose and release harmful substances. Here's how mechanical filters work:

- **How It Works:** Water flows through a filter medium (like sponge, foam, or mesh), which captures debris. The water then exits the filter, leaving the debris behind for easy removal. It is crucial to regularly clean or replace the filter medium to prevent clogging and ensure the system operates efficiently.

- **Importance:** Mechanical filtration helps reduce the load on biological filters by removing large particles, which could otherwise contribute to water contamination. It also prevents debris from settling at the bottom of the pond, where it can create murky water and increase the risk of diseases for koi.

- **Types of Mechanical Filters:** Skimmers and pre-filters are examples of mechanical filtration systems. Skimmers remove surface debris, while pre-filters work in conjunction with pumps to capture larger debris before the water passes through biological filters.

Biological Filtration

Biological filtration is essential for breaking down fish waste and other organic matter into less harmful compounds, ensuring water chemistry remains stable and safe for koi.

- **How It Works:** Biological filtration relies on beneficial bacteria that colonize the filter media. These bacteria convert toxic ammonia (produced by koi waste and decomposing matter) into nitrites, which are then further broken down into nitrates—a less harmful compound that can be absorbed by pond plants.

- **Importance:** Without biological filtration, ammonia and nitrites can quickly build up to dangerous levels, leading to fish stress, illness, or death. Biological filters maintain a natural nitrogen cycle, which is critical for koi's health.

- **Choosing Biological Filter Media:** Filter media designed for biological filtration, such as bio-balls, ceramic rings, or lava rocks, offer a large surface area for bacteria to thrive. Ensuring that your filtration system has adequate biological media is crucial, especially for heavily stocked koi ponds.

UV Sterilizers

UV sterilizers are an optional but beneficial addition to a koi pond filtration system. These devices help control algae growth and eliminate harmful pathogens from the water.

- **How It Works:** Water passes through a chamber containing a UV (ultraviolet) light bulb. The UV light destroys the DNA of algae cells and pathogens, preventing them from reproducing. As a result, algae blooms are reduced, and the water becomes clearer.

- **Benefits:** UV sterilizers help prevent green water caused by algae, improving the clarity and aesthetic of the pond. They also reduce the risk of koi disease by killing harmful bacteria and parasites. However, while UV sterilizers are effective against free-floating algae and pathogens, they don't address larger debris, so they should be used in conjunction with mechanical and biological filtration.

2.5.2 Pond Pumps

A high-quality pond pump is crucial for circulating water, ensuring proper filtration, and promoting oxygenation. Without adequate water movement, the pond can stagnate, leading to poor water quality and stress for your koi.

Types of Pond Pumps

Choosing the right pump depends on the size of your pond and the flow rate needed to maintain good water circulation.

- **Submersible Pumps:** These pumps are placed directly in the pond water, usually at the bottom. They are typically used for smaller ponds or water features. Submersible pumps are relatively easy to install and are generally quieter since they're submerged in water.

- **External Pumps:** External pumps are installed outside of the pond and are best suited for larger ponds or koi setups with complex filtration systems. Although they can be more expensive and louder than submersible pumps, they are often more energy-efficient and easier to maintain in the long run.

Selecting the Right Pump

- **Pond Size and Flow Rate:** As a general rule, the pump should circulate the entire volume of the pond at least once every hour or two. For example, if you have a 1,500-gallon pond, the pump should have a flow rate of 750–1,500 gallons per hour (GPH). Larger ponds or ponds with waterfalls and streams may require higher flow rates.

- **Energy Efficiency:** Since pond pumps run continuously, energy efficiency is an important consideration. Look for pumps with low energy consumption, especially if you're operating a large pond.

2.5.3 Aeration Systems

Aeration is critical to ensure that your koi pond has sufficient oxygen levels, especially during hot weather when oxygen can deplete quickly, or in deeper ponds where water circulation may be limited.

Types of Aeration Systems

- **Air Stones:** Air stones are placed at the bottom of the pond and connected to an air pump. They release fine bubbles into the water, helping to oxygenate and circulate the water. Air stones are ideal for small to medium-sized ponds.

- **Diffusers:** Diffusers work similarly to air stones but are more powerful and are typically used in larger or deeper ponds. They help distribute oxygen more evenly throughout the water.

- **Waterfalls and Fountains:** A decorative way to increase oxygenation is through the use of waterfalls or fountains. These features agitate the surface of the water, enhancing gas exchange and improving oxygen levels. In addition to aeration, they also help circulate water and add aesthetic value to the pond.

Importance of Aeration

Oxygenation: Koi require well-oxygenated water to thrive. Poor oxygen levels can lead to fish stress, disease, and even death in extreme cases. Aeration systems help ensure that dissolved oxygen is evenly distributed throughout the pond, particularly in deeper ponds where oxygen can be depleted at the bottom.

- **Prevents Stagnation:** In addition to oxygenation, aeration systems help prevent stagnation, which can lead to the buildup of harmful gases like carbon dioxide and hydrogen sulfide in the water.

2.5.4 Heaters and Temperature Control

In some climates, adding a pond heater may be necessary to regulate water temperature, especially during colder months when the pond is at risk of freezing.

When and Why Heaters Are Needed

- **Cold Climates:** If you live in a region with harsh winters, a pond heater can prevent the surface of the pond from freezing over completely, which would block gas exchange and potentially lead to fish death. A floating de-icer or pond heater ensures that a small area of the surface remains ice-free, allowing harmful gases to escape and oxygen to enter.

- **Preventing Temperature Stress:** Koi are sensitive to sudden temperature changes, especially when the water drops below 50°F (10°C). A heater can help maintain a stable temperature, preventing koi from experiencing stress during the winter.

Monitoring Water Temperature

- **Thermometers:** It's important to monitor the water temperature using a pond thermometer, especially during seasonal changes. By keeping a close eye on temperature fluctuations, you can make adjustments to the heating system as needed.

- **Ideal Temperature Range:** Koi prefer water temperatures between 65°F and 75°F (18°C to 24°C). If the water drops too far below this range, koi become sluggish and are at greater risk of illness. On the other hand, excessively warm water can reduce oxygen levels and lead to stress.

CHAPTER THREE

SETTING UP YOUR KOI POND

3.1 Creating the Ideal Water Environment

Maintaining a healthy water environment is critical for the well-being of koi. The quality of the water directly affects their health, growth, and behavior, so it's essential to monitor and regulate several key parameters. Understanding the fundamentals of water chemistry, temperature control, and proper water treatments can help ensure your koi thrive in a balanced ecosystem.

3.1.1 Water Quality Basics

The foundation of a healthy koi pond is high water quality, which involves monitoring and controlling several important water parameters. These parameters include pH, ammonia, nitrite, nitrate, dissolved oxygen, and water hardness. Regular testing and maintenance will keep these parameters in balance and provide a safe environment for your koi.

- **pH Levels:** The pH level measures the acidity or alkalinity of the water. Koi thrive in water with a pH range between 7.0 and 8.5. Keeping the pH within this range ensures the fish's biological processes function properly and prevents stress. A pH that is too low (acidic) or too high (alkaline) can weaken the immune system of koi, making them more susceptible to diseases.

pH Levels: Testing and Adjusting

- **Testing pH:** Use a reliable pH testing kit or digital meter to measure the pH of your pond water. It's important to test the pH regularly, especially after heavy rain, water changes, or adding new fish, as these factors can alter the water chemistry.

- **Adjusting pH:** If the pH is outside the desired range, you can adjust it using pH buffers or water conditioners. For low pH, adding baking soda or specialized pond pH stabilizers can raise the levels. If the pH is too high, you may need to add pH reducers or acid buffers. However, always make changes gradually to avoid shocking the koi with sudden fluctuations.

3.1.2 Ammonia, Nitrite, and Nitrate: The Nitrogen Cycle

Koi produce waste in the form of ammonia, which can be highly toxic to them. Understanding the nitrogen cycle is crucial for managing these toxins and maintaining a safe pond environment.

- **Ammonia:** This is the most toxic compound for koi, produced from fish waste, uneaten food, and decaying organic matter. Ammonia levels should always be at zero. Even low levels can cause stress, damage gills, and lead to diseases.

- **Nitrite:** Bacteria in the pond convert ammonia into nitrite, which is also harmful to koi. Nitrite interferes with the koi's ability to absorb oxygen, leading to suffocation even if oxygen levels in the water are sufficient. Nitrite levels, like ammonia, should be at zero.

- **Nitrate:** Nitrite is further broken down into nitrate by beneficial bacteria. Nitrate is less toxic but can lead to algae blooms if it builds up in the water. High nitrate levels can also stress koi over time, so it's recommended to keep them below 20 ppm. Plants in the pond can help absorb excess nitrates and maintain balance.

- **Managing the Nitrogen Cycle:** Proper biological filtration is essential to managing the nitrogen cycle. Beneficial bacteria colonize the filter media and convert ammonia and nitrite into less harmful nitrate. You can boost this process by adding beneficial bacteria supplements during the pond's initial setup or after cleaning.

3.1.3 Water Hardness (GH and KH)

Water hardness refers to the level of minerals, particularly calcium and magnesium, dissolved in the water. These minerals are essential for the health of koi and the stability of the pond environment.

- **General Hardness (GH):** GH measures the concentration of calcium and magnesium in the water. Koi need these minerals for proper growth and bone development. The ideal GH range for a koi pond is between 60 to 160 ppm. If the water is too soft (low GH), you can increase it by adding calcium carbonate or pond mineral blocks.

- **Carbonate Hardness (KH):** KH measures the water's ability to neutralize acids and maintain a stable pH. A stable KH level helps prevent pH swings, which can stress the koi. The recommended KH range is 100 to 200 ppm. You can increase KH by adding baking soda or KH buffers specifically designed for ponds.

3.1.4 Dissolved Oxygen

Koi need well-oxygenated water to thrive. Dissolved oxygen (DO) levels should be kept high to ensure the koi have enough oxygen for their metabolic processes. Oxygen levels can be affected by temperature, pond depth, and the number of fish.

- **Oxygen and Temperature:** Warm water holds less oxygen than cold water, so in the summer, oxygen levels can drop, leading to koi stress. In deeper ponds, oxygen levels may also decrease near the bottom if there's inadequate water circulation.

- **Aeration Systems:** Installing aeration devices such as air stones, diffusers, and waterfalls can help maintain adequate oxygen levels. Plants also play a role in oxygenating the water, particularly submerged plants that release oxygen into the water during the day.

- **Signs of Low Oxygen:** If koi are seen gasping at the surface or clustering near water sources with higher oxygen, it could be a sign that oxygen levels are too low. Address this immediately by increasing aeration.

3.1.5 Dechlorination and Water Treatments

If you're using tap water to fill or top up your pond, it's important to treat it before introducing it to the koi. Tap water often contains chlorine and chloramines, which are toxic to fish.

- **Dechlorination:** Use a dechlorinator or water conditioner to neutralize chlorine and chloramines before adding new water to the pond. These chemicals can irritate koi gills and lead to respiratory issues if left untreated.

- **Other Water Treatments:** In addition to dechlorinators, there are water treatments available to address specific issues like algae control, heavy metals, or bacterial imbalances. It's essential to read the instructions carefully and avoid overusing chemicals, as this can disrupt the pond's natural balance.

3.1.6 Water Changes and Regular Testing

Regular partial water changes are key to maintaining clean, healthy pond water. Water changes help dilute harmful compounds, refresh mineral content, and reduce the buildup of nitrates.

- **Frequency:** Aim for 10-20% weekly water changes. This helps maintain stable water parameters without shocking the koi with sudden changes.

- **Testing Water Parameters:** Invest in a high-quality water testing kit to monitor the pH, ammonia, nitrite, nitrate, GH, and KH levels regularly. Test the water weekly or more frequently if you notice any behavioral changes in the koi, such as erratic swimming or loss of appetite.

3.1.7 Temperature Control and Seasonality

Maintaining a consistent water temperature is important for koi, as sudden fluctuations can cause stress and weaken their immune systems.

- **Summer Heat:** During hot summers, high water temperatures can lower oxygen levels and increase stress on the fish. Providing shade with floating plants like water lilies, adding pond coolers, or installing shade cloths can help keep the water temperature stable. Ideal water temperature for koi is between 65°F and 75°F (18°C and 24°C).

- **Winter Cold:** In colder climates, freezing temperatures can create additional challenges. Koi are cold-blooded and will naturally become less active in the winter. It's important to prevent the water from freezing completely, which can cut off oxygen exchange and trap harmful gases.

- **Pond Heaters or De-icers:** A floating pond de-icer can keep a small area of the pond surface ice-free, allowing for gas exchange. In especially harsh winters, you may need to use a pond heater to maintain a safe temperature. However, koi can tolerate cold water if they are given a deep enough pond to retreat to the warmer lower layers.

- **Preventing Drastic Changes:** It's important to avoid rapid temperature changes by not filling the pond with water that is significantly warmer or colder than the current pond temperature. Gradual changes help koi acclimate without stress.

3.2 Introducing Beneficial Plants for Koi Ponds

Aquatic plants play a crucial role in maintaining a balanced and healthy ecosystem in a koi pond. They not only enhance the pond's aesthetics but also contribute significantly to water quality, koi health, and the overall pond environment. Incorporating the right mix of plants into your koi pond can reduce algae growth, provide shade, and create a more natural, dynamic habitat for your fish.

3.2.1 The Role of Plants in a Koi Pond

Aquatic plants offer multiple benefits that contribute to the health and vitality of a koi pond:

- **Nutrient Absorption:** Plants absorb excess nutrients like nitrogen and phosphates from fish waste, uneaten food, and decaying organic matter. By doing so, they help reduce the nutrient levels that fuel algae growth, thereby preventing harmful algae blooms.

- **Natural Filtration:** Many plants act as natural biofilters, removing toxins such as ammonia, nitrites, and heavy metals from the water. This process supports the biological filtration system and helps maintain clean, balanced water.

- **Oxygenation:** Some submerged plants oxygenate the water, helping maintain proper dissolved oxygen levels, which is crucial for koi health. They also assist with gas exchange, keeping the pond environment breathable for fish and other aquatic life.

- **Shade and Shelter:** Plants, especially floating and marginal varieties, provide shade, helping to regulate water temperature and reducing stress on koi during hot summer months. They also create natural hiding spots for young koi, protecting them from predators and giving them a sense of security.

- **Aesthetic Appeal:** In addition to their practical benefits, aquatic plants enhance the visual appeal of a koi pond, adding natural beauty, texture, and color. Their presence can transform a simple water feature into a lush, vibrant ecosystem.

3.2.2 Floating Plants for Koi Ponds

Floating plants are not anchored in the soil but instead float freely on the pond's surface. They are particularly effective at shading the water, which helps reduce algae growth, cool the water temperature, and limit direct sunlight exposure.

- **Water Lettuce (Pistia stratiotes):** Known for its attractive floating rosettes of velvety, pale green leaves, water lettuce is a favorite in koi ponds. It absorbs excess nutrients from the water and creates dense shade, which helps cool the water and reduce algae growth. Water lettuce is also a low-maintenance plant, making it ideal for beginner pond keepers.

- **Water Hyacinth (Eichhornia crassipes):** Water hyacinth is a fast-growing floating plant with delicate lavender flowers. It is highly effective at improving water quality by absorbing nitrates and phosphates. However, it can spread quickly and may require regular thinning to prevent overcrowding, especially in warmer climates. Care should be taken not to let it overrun the pond.

- **Duckweed (Lemna minor):** Duckweed is a tiny, rapidly growing plant that forms a green carpet over the pond's surface. It provides excellent cover for the pond, blocking sunlight and thus preventing algae blooms. Duckweed is also a nutritious snack for koi, though it can proliferate rapidly, so it needs to be controlled to avoid excessive coverage.

3.2.3 Submerged Plants for Koi Ponds

Submerged plants, also known as oxygenators, grow entirely beneath the water's surface. These plants play an important role in oxygenating the water, providing hiding spaces for fish, and absorbing nutrients that would otherwise promote algae growth.

- **Anacharis (Elodea canadensis):** Anacharis, or Elodea, is a common submerged plant that helps oxygenate the water and improves overall pond health. It grows quickly, absorbing excess nutrients and preventing algae from flourishing. Additionally, its dense, feathery leaves provide koi with hiding spots and protect young fish from predators.

- **Hornwort (Ceratophyllum demersum):** Hornwort is a hardy, fast-growing submerged plant that thrives in a variety of conditions. It oxygenates the pond water while also acting as a nutrient sponge, absorbing nitrates and phosphates that can otherwise lead to algae growth. Hornwort is also popular because koi are less likely to nibble on it, making it an excellent choice for a koi pond.

3.2.4 Marginal Plants for Koi Ponds

Marginal plants grow around the edges of the pond, with their roots submerged and their foliage above the waterline. These plants help prevent erosion, act as natural filters, and enhance the pond's visual appeal.

- **Iris (Iris spp.):** Irises are marginal plants that thrive in the shallow waters along the edges of ponds. Their stunning flowers add a splash of color to the pond landscape, while their strong root systems help prevent soil erosion. Irises also act as a natural filter, absorbing nutrients and improving water quality.

- **Cattails (Typha spp.):** Cattails are tall, iconic plants that add vertical interest to a pond's landscape. Beyond their aesthetics, cattails are also highly functional—they absorb excess nutrients from the water, helping to keep the pond clean. Their roots create a dense network that helps reduce erosion and stabilize the pond's edges.

- **Lotus (Nelumbo nucifera) and Water Lilies (Nymphaea spp.):** Lotus and water lilies are two of the most popular plants for koi ponds. Water lilies are renowned for their floating, colorful flowers, which provide shade for koi, helping regulate water temperature and create hiding spots. Lotus plants have larger, more dramatic blooms and can reach impressive heights, adding an exotic touch to the pond. Both plants' large leaves offer significant shade, cooling the pond and suppressing algae growth.

3.2.5 Balancing Plant and Fish Needs

Koi have a tendency to nibble on plants, especially tender, young shoots. While plants are beneficial for the pond environment, balancing their needs with the koi's habits is essential.

- **Protecting Plants:** To prevent koi from uprooting or damaging plants, consider using floating barriers or plant pots. Planting in pots allows you to position the plants strategically around the pond while also protecting their roots from being disturbed. Additionally, submerged plants like Anacharis can be weighted down or anchored in place using rocks or plant weights.

- **Introducing Hardy Plants:** Opt for hardy, robust plant species that can withstand koi nibbling. Plants like hornwort and water lilies are more resilient and can tolerate occasional nibbling from koi without suffering significant damage.

- **Balancing Growth:** Regular pruning and thinning of fast-growing plants like duckweed and water hyacinth will ensure that they don't overcrowd the pond or block too much light. Maintaining a balance between plant coverage and open water is important for both the health of the koi and the pond's overall ecosystem.

3.3 Choosing Rocks, Gravel, and Other Decorative Elements

Incorporating rocks, gravel, and other decorative elements into your koi pond not only enhances its visual appeal but also serves practical purposes that contribute to the overall health and functionality of the pond. These natural materials help create a balanced ecosystem by promoting beneficial bacteria growth, improving water filtration, and providing shelter for koi. Thoughtful selection and placement of these elements can transform a simple pond into a stunning, thriving habitat for your fish.

3.3.1 The Benefits of Rocks and Gravel

Rocks and gravel offer both aesthetic and functional advantages to a koi pond:

- **Natural Look and Feel:** Rocks and gravel mimic the natural environment of ponds and streams, giving your koi pond a more organic and inviting appearance. They can help create a harmonious transition between the pond and surrounding landscape.

- **Anchoring Plants:** Rocks and gravel are useful for stabilizing aquatic plants, especially marginal or submerged varieties. They provide a stable surface for planting, preventing plants from floating away or being uprooted by koi.

- **Surface for Beneficial Bacteria:** Both rocks and gravel provide a large surface area for beneficial bacteria to colonize. These bacteria play a crucial role in the nitrogen cycle, breaking down harmful ammonia and nitrites produced by fish waste and decaying organic matter into less harmful nitrates. This natural filtration process helps maintain clean, healthy water for your koi.

- **Erosion Control:** Placing rocks along the pond's edges can help prevent soil erosion, especially in areas where the water meets land. This is particularly beneficial for ponds with sloped sides or in regions prone to heavy rainfall.

3.3.2 Choosing Safe Rocks for Your Koi Pond

Selecting the right type of rock is critical to ensuring the safety and health of your koi. Some rocks can leach harmful chemicals or minerals into the water, altering its chemistry and potentially harming your fish.

- **River Rocks:** River rocks are smooth, rounded stones that have been naturally shaped by the flow of water. They are commonly used in koi ponds because they are safe, non-toxic, and add a natural aesthetic. Their smooth surfaces also minimize the risk of injuring koi as they swim close to the bottom or edges of the pond.

- **Basalt and Granite:** Both basalt and granite are volcanic rocks that are durable and safe for koi ponds. They are less likely to affect the water's pH levels and can withstand weathering and temperature fluctuations. Basalt is often used for creating dramatic waterfalls or stepping stones due to its dark color and sleek appearance, while granite can be used to line the pond's perimeter or form underwater ledges.

- **Avoid Limestone:** While limestone is a common decorative rock, it should be avoided in koi ponds.

Limestone is rich in calcium carbonate, which can dissolve into the pond water and cause the pH to rise. A higher pH level can stress koi and disrupt the pond's ecosystem. It's important to stick with inert rocks that won't alter water chemistry.

- **Thorough Cleaning:** Regardless of the type of rock you choose, it's essential to thoroughly clean all rocks before placing them in the pond. Rocks can carry dirt, dust, algae, and other contaminants that could cloud the water or introduce harmful substances. Scrub them with water and a brush to remove surface debris, and avoid using any chemicals or detergents that could leave toxic residues.

3.3.3 Placement and Aesthetic Considerations

The strategic placement of rocks and gravel can significantly enhance both the appearance and functionality of your koi pond. Consider the following when positioning these elements:

- **Creating Visual Depth:** Use rocks of varying sizes to create depth and visual interest. Larger rocks can be placed near the pond's edges to define the perimeter, while smaller rocks and gravel can be used to create natural transitions between deeper and shallower areas.

- **Waterfalls and Cascades:** Rocks are often used to create waterfalls, cascades, or streams within a pond. These features not only add aesthetic beauty but also serve functional purposes by enhancing water movement and oxygenation, which is beneficial for koi health. Position flat stones or boulders in layers to create natural-looking waterfalls, allowing water to flow smoothly and aerate the pond.

- **Enhancing Water Flow:** When placing rocks, ensure they don't impede water flow. Proper circulation is essential for maintaining a healthy pond, as it distributes oxygen and prevents stagnation. If using rocks to build ledges or steps, leave enough space between them to allow water to move freely.

- **Hiding Equipment:** Large rocks can be used to conceal unsightly pond equipment, such as pumps, filters, or skimmers, without obstructing their functionality. This helps maintain the pond's natural look while ensuring the equipment remains accessible for maintenance.

3.3.4 Creating Hiding Spots and Shelters

Koi need areas where they can retreat and seek shelter, especially from predators or during hot weather. Rocks can be arranged to form caves, tunnels, and shaded spots that offer koi a sense of security and reduce stress.

- **Cave Structures:** Large, flat rocks or boulders can be placed on top of smaller rocks to create caves or overhangs. These structures provide koi with shaded areas to hide during the day, especially if the pond receives a lot of sunlight. Caves also serve as protection from potential predators like birds or cats.

- **Tunnels and Sheltered Spaces:** Use rocks to form tunnels or sheltered spaces along the pond's bottom, allowing koi to swim through and explore. These structures simulate the koi's natural environment and help reduce stress by giving them safe, enclosed spaces.

3.3.5 Gravel for the Pond Bottom

Using gravel at the bottom of the pond can enhance its appearance and provide practical benefits, but it comes with both advantages and challenges.

- **Promoting Beneficial Bacteria:** Like rocks, gravel provides a surface for beneficial bacteria to colonize. These bacteria help process fish waste and other organic matter, contributing to the pond's natural filtration system. Gravel can be particularly useful in promoting the growth of these bacteria at the pond's bottom, where waste tends to accumulate.

- **Aesthetic Appeal:** Gravel gives the pond bottom a clean, finished look and can be used to complement the colors and textures of surrounding rocks and plants. It also helps anchor plants and keep them from floating to the surface.

- **Potential for Debris Trapping:** While gravel is beneficial for bacterial colonization, it can also trap debris, such as fish waste, uneaten food, and decaying plant material. Over time, this debris can break down and release harmful substances like ammonia, negatively affecting water quality. Regular cleaning or the use of a pond vacuum is essential to prevent debris buildup.

- **Maintenance Tips:** If you choose to use gravel, consider installing it in areas of the pond with good water circulation, where debris is less likely to settle. Alternatively, you can limit gravel to plant pots or specific areas, leaving other parts of the pond bare for easier cleaning.

3.4 Adding Lighting for Ambience and Fish Health

Lighting in koi ponds serves a dual purpose: it enhances the visual appeal of the pond, particularly at night, and offers subtle benefits for fish health and water quality. While koi do not require artificial light to thrive, thoughtfully placed lighting can transform a pond into a striking centerpiece during the evening, allowing you to enjoy its beauty after dark. Careful consideration of the type, intensity, and placement of lights ensures that the pond remains visually stunning without disrupting the health and well-being of the koi.

3.4.1 The Role of Lighting in Koi Ponds

Lighting plays an essential role in the aesthetic experience of a koi pond. It adds a magical atmosphere after sunset, accentuating the pond's features and showcasing the koi's vibrant colors as they glide through the water. However, lighting can also offer practical benefits, such as enhancing safety around the pond at night and helping with water clarity through UV treatments.

- **Enhancing Aesthetics:** Lighting allows pond owners to enjoy their koi even after dark. By illuminating the water, rocks, and plants, lighting highlights the pond's natural beauty and creates a captivating display. It can be used to showcase specific features like waterfalls, fountains, or decorative statues, turning the pond into a focal point during evening gatherings or quiet nights outdoors.

- **Supporting Koi Health:** While koi do not need artificial lighting to live, ambient light levels can subtly influence their behavior and stress levels. Overly harsh or bright lights can stress koi, so it's important to use soft, ambient lighting that mimics the calming effects of natural moonlight. UV lights also contribute to fish health indirectly by reducing algae growth and keeping water clear, which supports a healthier environment for the koi.

Types of Pond Lighting

There are several types of lighting that can be used to create a balanced, aesthetically pleasing, and functional lighting system for koi ponds:

1. Underwater Lighting

- **Submerged LED or Halogen Lights:** These lights are installed underwater to illuminate koi as they swim. LED lights are preferred for their energy efficiency and ability to emit a strong yet soft glow without overheating the pond water. They are perfect for highlighting the koi's vibrant scales at night, creating a dynamic and engaging visual experience.

- **Light Placement:** Place underwater lights in areas where koi are most active, such as near feeding zones or deeper swimming areas. Submerged lights should be positioned carefully to avoid shining directly into the fish's eyes, which can cause stress.

2. Floating Lights

- **Solar-Powered Floating Lights:** These lights float on the water's surface, providing a soft, warm glow that enhances the pond's ambiance. Since they are solar-powered, they are eco-friendly and require minimal maintenance, recharging during the day and illuminating the pond at night without the need for electrical wiring.

- **Decorative Appeal:** Floating lights are particularly appealing for those seeking a whimsical or relaxed atmosphere. They move gently with the water, creating dynamic reflections that add depth and interest to the pond's surface.

3. Spotlights and Pathway Lighting

- **Spotlights:** Spotlights are versatile and can be used to highlight specific features around the pond, such as waterfalls, fountains, statues, or large rocks. When angled correctly, they can cast dramatic shadows or reflections on the pond's surface, enhancing the overall visual experience.

- **Pathway Lighting:** Pathway lighting around the pond enhances both safety and aesthetics. It ensures that the area is well-lit for evening strolls, reducing the risk of accidents, while also adding to the overall ambiance. Low-profile pathway lights can be used to subtly guide visitors around the pond without overpowering the natural beauty of the space.

3.4.2 Lighting for Fish Health

When choosing lighting for a koi pond, it's important to consider how different light intensities and colors affect the koi. Koi are sensitive to changes in their environment, and lighting can have both positive and negative effects on their well-being.

- **Natural Light Cycles:** Koi naturally respond to changes in light, so it's important to avoid lighting that is too intense or disruptive. Harsh, bright lights, especially those that remain on throughout the night, can confuse koi and increase their stress levels. Instead, opt for soft, warm lighting that mimics the gradual changes in natural light at dawn or dusk.

- **Ambient Lighting:** Soft, ambient lighting around the pond's perimeter or within the water helps create a soothing environment for koi. It is important to choose lights that do not produce strong glares or direct beams into the water, as this can disturb the koi's natural rhythms.

- **UV Lighting for Algae Control:** UV sterilizers can be integrated into the pond's filtration system to help control algae growth. While these lights do not add to the visual appeal of the pond, they serve a practical purpose by maintaining water clarity and reducing the risk of harmful pathogens. Clearer water not only benefits the koi's health but also improves visibility, allowing the koi to be better appreciated even at night.

3.4.3 Creating a Balanced Lighting Scheme

Creating a harmonious balance between functional and decorative lighting is key to maintaining both the health of the koi and the pond's visual appeal. Here are some tips for achieving a balanced lighting design:

- **Avoiding Harsh Glare and Shadows:** Lights should be positioned in such a way that they enhance the pond's features without creating harsh glares on the water's surface or casting unflattering shadows. Experiment with the angles and placement of lights to find the right balance of illumination and shadow play.

- **Highlighting Key Features:** Use spotlights or submerged lights to draw attention to key elements of the pond, such as koi, plants, or rock formations. Color-changing LED lights can add a playful touch, but they should be used sparingly to avoid overwhelming the natural aesthetic of the pond.

- **Subtle Illumination:** A good rule of thumb is to aim for subtlety rather than brightness. Use dimmer, more focused lighting to softly illuminate areas where koi swim and feed, allowing their natural colors to be highlighted without the need for overly intense lighting.

Solar vs. Electric Lighting

Pond lighting systems can be powered by either solar energy or electricity, each with its own advantages and limitations.

Solar-Powered Lighting

- **Eco-Friendly and Cost-Effective:** Solar lights are an environmentally friendly option, harnessing the sun's energy during the day to power the lights at night. This makes them a low-cost, low-maintenance choice for those who want to reduce their energy consumption.

- **Limitations:** The downside to solar lighting is that it may not provide consistent illumination, especially on cloudy or rainy days. Solar-powered lights also tend to be less bright than electrically powered ones, which may be a limitation if you need more powerful lighting for larger ponds.

Electric Lighting

- **Greater Flexibility and Brightness Control:** Electric lighting systems are more reliable and provide greater control over brightness and color settings. They are especially suitable for larger ponds that require consistent, powerful illumination.

- **Higher Installation and Maintenance Costs:** While electric lighting offers more flexibility, it comes with higher installation costs, as wiring and electrical connections need to be established around the pond. Regular maintenance may also be required to keep the system running efficiently.

CHAPTER FOUR

WATER QUALITY AND MAINTENANCE

4.1 The Importance of Clean, Oxygenated Water

A koi pond's success depends heavily on maintaining clean, oxygen-rich water. Koi are highly sensitive to water quality, and even slight imbalances can lead to stress, disease, or death. Achieving the right balance between clarity, oxygenation, and chemistry is essential to provide koi with a healthy and stable environment.

4.1.1 Water Quality for Koi Health

While clear water is visually appealing, it is not necessarily an indicator of good water quality. Many harmful substances—such as ammonia, nitrite, and nitrates—are invisible, making it important to focus on both water clarity and chemistry.

- **Impact on Koi Health:** Poor water quality puts koi under significant stress, weakening their immune systems and making them more susceptible to diseases. Excessive waste, uneaten food, and decaying organic matter in the water can lead to the accumulation of toxic substances like ammonia and nitrite, which are harmful even in small amounts. Maintaining water quality through proper filtration and regular testing ensures that the pond remains a safe and thriving environment for koi.

- **Key Water Parameters:** In addition to keeping the water free of debris, you must regularly test critical water parameters such as pH, ammonia, nitrite, nitrate, and dissolved oxygen levels. The balance of these elements directly impacts the health of the fish and the stability of the pond's ecosystem.

4.1.2 The Role of Oxygenation

Dissolved oxygen is crucial for koi and the overall health of the pond. Koi, like all fish, breathe by extracting oxygen from the water through their gills. A lack of oxygen can lead to respiratory stress, lethargy, or even death. In addition to being essential for koi, oxygen is necessary for the survival of beneficial bacteria that break down waste in the pond.

- **Oxygen for Beneficial Bacteria:** The bacteria in the pond's filtration system rely on oxygen to process harmful substances like ammonia and nitrite into less toxic nitrate. Without adequate oxygen levels, these bacteria cannot function properly, which may lead to spikes in ammonia or nitrite that can be lethal to koi. This makes oxygenation not only vital for the koi's health but also for maintaining water quality.

- **Stable Ecosystem:** A well-oxygenated pond promotes a healthy ecosystem where koi, plants, and bacteria coexist harmoniously. Plants and bacteria rely on dissolved oxygen for respiration, while koi benefit from the cleaner, more stable environment created by efficient biological filtration.

4.1.3 Factors Affecting Oxygen Levels

Oxygen levels in a pond are not static and can fluctuate based on several factors, including temperature, depth, and water movement.

- **Temperature:** Warmer water holds less oxygen than cooler water, which is why oxygen depletion is more common during hot summer months. As water temperature rises, the oxygen demand of koi increases, but the water's capacity to hold oxygen decreases, leading to potential stress or suffocation for the fish if oxygen levels drop too low.

- **Water Depth:** Deeper ponds often have lower oxygen levels at the bottom because water movement and circulation may not reach those depths. This can lead to the formation of "dead zones" where oxygen is scarce, making these areas uninhabitable for koi and other pond life.

- **Water Movement:** Stagnant water can lead to low oxygen levels, especially in warm weather. Without proper circulation, dissolved oxygen may not be evenly distributed throughout the pond, leading to pockets of low-oxygen water where koi may struggle to breathe. Additionally, stagnant water promotes the buildup of waste and debris, further degrading water quality.

4.1.4 Methods of Aeration

Maintaining high oxygen levels is essential for a healthy koi pond, and various aeration methods can help increase oxygenation and water circulation.

- **Air Pumps:** Air pumps deliver oxygen directly to the pond by pushing air through diffusers placed at the pond's bottom. As the air bubbles rise, they increase water movement and dissolve oxygen into the water, creating a more oxygen-rich environment. Air pumps are particularly useful in deeper ponds where circulation may be limited at the bottom.

- **Diffusers:** Diffusers are used in conjunction with air pumps to spread oxygen more evenly throughout the pond. By breaking air into smaller bubbles, diffusers increase the surface area of the oxygen that comes into contact with the water, making the oxygenation process more efficient.

- **Waterfalls:** A well-designed waterfall not only adds beauty and tranquility to the pond but also serves as an effective aeration tool. As water cascades down the rocks, it captures oxygen from the air and distributes it throughout the pond. Waterfalls are particularly beneficial for larger ponds, as they increase water movement and oxygenation while also providing visual appeal.

- **Fountains:** Like waterfalls, fountains increase water movement and help with oxygenation. They can be placed in the middle of the pond to create a dramatic focal point while keeping the water circulating. Fountains can be equipped with aerators that ensure constant water movement, preventing stagnation.

- **Surface Agitation:** Encouraging water movement at the surface can also promote oxygen exchange. Aeration devices or even strategic placement of pond pumps can agitate the surface, facilitating the exchange of gases (oxygen and carbon dioxide) between the water and the air.

4.1.5 Benefits of Proper Circulation

Water circulation is not only important for oxygenation but also for maintaining a healthy, stable pond environment. Proper water movement ensures that oxygen is evenly distributed throughout the pond and prevents the formation of stagnant zones where waste and debris can accumulate.

- **Oxygen Distribution:** With the help of pumps, aerators, and other circulation devices, water is constantly moving, ensuring that oxygen reaches all areas of the pond. This is especially important in ponds with varying depths, where stagnant, oxygen-poor zones could otherwise develop at the bottom.

- **Prevention of Dead Zones:** Without proper circulation, some areas of the pond may become stagnant and low in oxygen, creating dead zones that are inhospitable to koi and beneficial bacteria. These dead zones also allow waste and organic debris to settle and decompose, potentially releasing harmful substances back into the water.

- **Waste Management:** Moving water helps to keep debris suspended, allowing it to be filtered out more efficiently. In a well-circulated pond, fish waste, uneaten food, and other organic matter are less likely to settle at the bottom and accumulate into harmful sludge. This leads to a cleaner, healthier pond environment for koi.

- **Temperature Regulation:** Proper circulation helps regulate water temperature by distributing cooler or warmer water throughout the pond. This prevents temperature stratification, where the water near the surface becomes much warmer than the deeper layers. Uneven temperatures can stress koi, but consistent water movement helps maintain a stable, comfortable environment for the fish.

4.2 Understanding pH Levels, Ammonia, Nitrite, and Nitrate

Maintaining optimal water chemistry is essential for ensuring a healthy environment for koi. Water chemistry imbalances, especially in terms of pH, ammonia, nitrite, and nitrate levels, can cause stress, illness, or even death in koi. Regular monitoring and timely corrective actions are vital to keeping your koi thriving. Here's a detailed look at these key water parameters and how to manage them effectively.

4.2.1 Monitoring Water Chemistry

Regular monitoring of water chemistry is one of the most important tasks for any koi pond owner. Test kits are readily available and should be used frequently to track levels of pH, ammonia, nitrite, and nitrate. Ideally, you should test the water weekly and after any significant changes to the pond (like water changes, heavy rainfall, or the addition of new fish). Keeping a log of your test results allows you to detect patterns and make adjustments as needed before imbalances become severe.

- **Actionable Steps:** When water parameters become unbalanced, immediate action should be taken. For example, high ammonia or nitrite levels require quick intervention, such as increased filtration, partial water changes, or reducing feeding to prevent further water quality degradation. Waiting too long can result in significant stress or harm to koi.

pH Levels: The Foundation of Water Chemistry

The pH level of the water refers to its acidity or alkalinity, and maintaining a stable pH is crucial for the well-being of koi. Koi thrive in slightly alkaline water, with an ideal pH range of 7.0 to 8.5. Water outside this range can stress the fish and disrupt the effectiveness of biological filtration.

- **pH Fluctuations:** Rapid fluctuations in pH are particularly dangerous for koi, as they can lead to stress and compromise the fish's immune system. Even if the pH stays within the acceptable range, drastic shifts from day to night or after heavy rain can still harm your koi. Pond owners should aim to maintain stable pH levels by monitoring regularly and avoiding any drastic changes.

- **Maintaining Stable pH:** A stable pH can be achieved using natural buffers. Crushed oyster shells or coral can be added to the pond or the filter system to buffer the pH and keep it stable.

Baking soda can also be used in small amounts to raise the pH if it falls below 7. However, any adjustments should be made gradually to avoid shocking the koi. Rainwater, which is typically more acidic, can lower pH levels during rainy seasons, so it's important to monitor the water closely after significant rainfall.

4.2.2 Ammonia: A Silent but Deadly Toxin

Ammonia is one of the most toxic substances in a koi pond and is primarily produced by fish waste, decaying organic matter, and uneaten food. Even at low levels, ammonia can cause severe harm to koi, damaging their gills and making it difficult for them to breathe. It also weakens their immune system, making them more susceptible to disease.

- **Ammonia Toxicity:** Ammonia is particularly harmful because it disrupts the koi's ability to absorb oxygen. Koi exposed to high levels of ammonia often exhibit lethargy, gasping at the surface, or signs of gill damage (red, inflamed gills). In the worst cases, prolonged exposure can lead to death.

- **Ammonia Control:** The most effective way to manage ammonia levels is through proper biological filtration. Beneficial bacteria in the pond's filtration system break down ammonia into nitrite, which is less toxic. To prevent ammonia buildup, avoid overfeeding the koi, as uneaten food contributes significantly to ammonia production. Regular cleaning of the pond and filter system to remove decaying organic matter is also critical.

4.2.3 Nitrite: A Harmful Byproduct

As part of the nitrogen cycle, ammonia is converted into nitrite by beneficial bacteria. Although nitrite is less toxic than ammonia, it is still dangerous to koi, particularly in high concentrations. Nitrite poisoning can lead to a condition known as brown blood disease, where koi's blood turns brown because it can no longer effectively transport oxygen.

- **Signs of Nitrite Poisoning:** Koi suffering from high nitrite levels may become lethargic, lose appetite, or gasp for air at the water's surface. Brown blood disease occurs because nitrite interferes with the hemoglobin in the blood, preventing it from carrying oxygen efficiently.

- **Converting Nitrite to Nitrate:** Nitrite is further broken down into nitrate by another set of beneficial bacteria in the biological filtration system. This conversion is a natural and essential process in a healthy pond ecosystem. To ensure efficient nitrite breakdown, it's important to maintain a healthy population of beneficial bacteria. This means cleaning the filter system regularly but not too aggressively, as scrubbing away all the bacteria can disrupt the nitrogen cycle.

Nitrate: The Least Harmful but Still a Concern

Nitrate is the final byproduct in the nitrogen cycle and is significantly less toxic to koi than ammonia or nitrite. However, high nitrate levels can still cause long-term health issues for koi and lead to excessive algae growth, which can deplete oxygen levels in the pond.

- **Managing Nitrate Levels:** The best way to manage nitrate levels is through regular water changes. Performing partial water changes (10-20% weekly) helps dilute nitrates and prevent them from accumulating. Additionally, introducing aquatic plants into the pond can be an effective way to naturally reduce nitrates. Plants like water lilies, hornwort, and other submerged or floating species absorb nitrates as nutrients, helping to keep levels in check while also improving the overall aesthetic of the pond.

4.2.4 Practical Tips for Maintaining Water Chemistry Balance

- **Regular Testing:** Investing in a reliable water test kit is essential for monitoring pH, ammonia, nitrite, and nitrate levels. Regular testing allows you to spot issues before they become severe and take proactive steps to maintain a balanced environment for your koi.

- **Feeding Practices:** Overfeeding is a common cause of ammonia and nitrite spikes. Feed your koi only what they can eat in a few minutes, and remove any uneaten food from the pond. Excess food not only leads to ammonia production but also promotes algae growth, which can further degrade water quality.

- **Biological Filtration:** Ensuring that your biological filter is working efficiently is key to keeping ammonia, nitrite, and nitrate levels under control. This involves maintaining a balance between cleaning the filter to remove debris and allowing beneficial bacteria to thrive. Avoid using harsh chemicals or excessive cleaning, as this can kill off the bacteria essential for the nitrogen cycle.

- **Water Changes:** Regular water changes are critical for maintaining water quality. They help reduce the buildup of harmful substances like ammonia and nitrate, as well as refresh the pond with oxygen-rich water. Changing 10-20% of the water each week is generally recommended for optimal pond health.

- **Plant Integration:** Introducing aquatic plants into the pond provides natural filtration, absorbing excess nutrients like nitrate and preventing algae overgrowth. Plants also provide shade and shelter for koi, making them a valuable addition to any koi pond.

4.3 Regular Pond Cleaning and Maintenance Schedule

A well-maintained koi pond not only enhances the aesthetic appeal of your outdoor space but also ensures a healthy, thriving environment for your koi. Routine maintenance helps prevent water quality issues, algae blooms, and potential health problems for the fish.

4.3.1 The Importance of Routine Maintenance

Routine maintenance is crucial for preventing problems before they escalate. Neglecting pond upkeep can result in poor water quality, which stresses the fish and weakens their immune system, leading to disease outbreaks. Algae blooms, buildup of harmful toxins like ammonia, and equipment malfunction can all be avoided with regular care. Proactively managing the pond reduces the need for costly repairs or emergency interventions down the road.

4.3.2 Daily and Weekly Tasks: A Practical Maintenance Schedule

Here's a detailed breakdown of tasks to perform on a daily, weekly, and monthly basis, designed to keep your pond in optimal condition with minimal effort.

1. Daily Maintenance Tasks

Check Water Temperature

- **Why:** Water temperature directly affects koi metabolism and oxygen levels. Koi thrive best between 65°F and 75°F (18°C to 24°C). Temperatures outside this range can cause stress or illness.

- **What to Do:** Use a pond thermometer to check the water temperature daily. If it gets too hot, consider providing additional shade or increasing aeration. For colder weather, be mindful of ice formation in winter, which can block gas exchange.

Ensure Equipment is Functioning Properly

- **Why:** Pumps, filters, and aerators are vital for circulating water, maintaining oxygen levels, and ensuring good water quality.

- **What to Do:** Check that pumps and filters are operating smoothly. Look for signs of malfunction, such as unusual noises, reduced water flow, or air bubbles. Address any issues immediately to prevent oxygen depletion or water stagnation.

Inspect for Debris

- **Why:** Organic matter like leaves, dead plant material, and uneaten food can degrade water quality by producing ammonia as they decompose.

- **What to Do:** Skim the surface of the pond to remove any floating debris. Pay attention to corners and crevices where waste might accumulate. Promptly remove any decaying matter to reduce the risk of ammonia buildup.

Feed Koi an Appropriate Amount

- **Why:** Overfeeding leads to excess waste in the pond, which increases ammonia and nitrate levels, harming water quality.

- **What to Do:** Feed the koi only what they can consume within 5 minutes. Remove any uneaten food immediately after feeding. Adjust feeding frequency based on water temperature, reducing food during colder months when koi metabolism slows down.

2. Weekly Maintenance Tasks

Test Water Parameters

- **Why:** Regularly testing water ensures that pH, ammonia, nitrite, and nitrate levels remain within safe ranges. Fluctuations can stress koi and lead to health problems.

- **What to Do:** Use a test kit to monitor key parameters. The ideal ranges are:
- **pH:** 7.0 to 8.5
- **Ammonia:** 0 ppm (parts per million)
- **Nitrite:** 0 ppm
- **Nitrate:** Less than 50 ppm

If levels are off, take corrective measures such as performing a water change or adjusting the biological filter.

Perform Partial Water Change (10-20%)

- **Why:** Regular water changes dilute toxins like nitrates and help refresh the pond environment.
- **What to Do:** Drain 10-20% of the pond water and replace it with dechlorinated, temperature-matched fresh water. Ensure the new water is the

same temperature as the pond to avoid stressing the fish. This helps keep nitrate levels low and restores oxygen balance.

Rinse Mechanical Filters

- **Why:** Filters trap debris, but over time, they can become clogged and lose efficiency, leading to poor water circulation.

- **What to Do:** Rinse out mechanical filter pads in a bucket of pond water (not tap water) to remove debris without killing beneficial bacteria. Clean just enough to restore flow, avoiding over-cleaning to preserve good bacteria.

Check for Algae Growth

- **Why:** Excessive algae not only looks unattractive but can also lead to oxygen depletion at night and produce toxins harmful to koi.

- **What to Do:** Look for algae buildup on the pond's surface, rocks, and plant roots. If algae are present, consider reducing feeding, increasing shade, or adding aquatic plants that compete with algae for nutrients. In some cases, an algae control treatment may be necessary, but avoid harsh chemicals that could harm koi.

3. Monthly Maintenance Tasks

Inspect Pond Liners, Rocks, and Equipment

- **Why:** Wear and tear can cause leaks, equipment failure, or structural damage, all of which affect pond performance.
- **What to Do:** Check pond liners for punctures or tears, rocks for shifting or erosion, and equipment for signs of damage. If you notice any issues, make repairs or replacements as necessary. A leak can

lead to water loss and increased pressure on filtration systems.

Clean Biological Filters Carefully

- **Why:** Biological filters house beneficial bacteria that break down ammonia and nitrite, keeping the pond water safe for koi.

- **What to Do:** Clean biological filters sparingly and always use pond water to avoid killing off beneficial bacteria. Clean only when the flow is noticeably reduced, and be gentle in handling filter media. Never sterilize the filter.

Prune Aquatic Plants

- **Why:** Overgrown plants can block sunlight, clog filters, and restrict water flow, reducing oxygen levels in the pond.

- **What to Do:** Trim any overgrown or dead plant material to ensure proper light penetration and water circulation. Be sure to remove any plant debris from the pond to prevent it from decomposing and contributing to nutrient buildup.

Inspect Koi for Health Issues

- **Why:** Regular health checks can catch problems like parasites, injuries, or infections early, preventing them from becoming more serious.

- **What to Do:** Take time to observe the koi's behavior and appearance. Look for any signs of illness, such as lethargy, gasping at the surface, fin damage, or visible parasites. If you notice anything unusual, isolate the affected fish and consult a vet or koi specialist.

Thorough Pond Cleaning (If Necessary)

- **Why:** Over time, sediment, organic waste, and other debris can accumulate at the bottom of the pond, leading to water quality issues.

- **What to Do:** If there's significant debris buildup, perform a more thorough cleaning. Use a pond vacuum or manually remove debris from the bottom of the pond. Be cautious not to disturb the beneficial bacteria too much. Large cleanups should be done in small sections to avoid shocking the pond's ecosystem.

4.4 Dealing with Algae and Pond Pests

Maintaining a koi pond involves not only caring for the fish but also managing the pond's ecosystem, including algae and various pests that can impact water quality and fish health. While some algae are beneficial, excessive growth or pests can quickly turn into problems that disrupt the delicate balance of the pond.

4.4.1 Algae: Friend or Foe?

Algae play a dual role in the koi pond environment. On one hand, they are a natural part of any pond ecosystem and can even provide a food source for koi. In small amounts, algae contribute to the balance of the pond by helping to oxygenate the water during the day and offering grazing opportunities for the fish. However, when algae grow unchecked, they can become a nuisance, causing poor water quality and potentially harming koi.

The Harmful Effects of Excessive Algae

- **Oxygen Depletion:** Algae consume oxygen at night when photosynthesis ceases, potentially leading to low oxygen levels in the water, especially in warm weather when koi already need more oxygen.

- **Blocking Sunlight:** Excessive algae, particularly string algae, can block sunlight from reaching submerged plants and disrupt their ability to produce oxygen through photosynthesis. In turn, this can affect the overall health of the pond ecosystem.

- **Aesthetic Issues:** Algae overgrowth often causes the pond water to look murky or green, detracting from the visual appeal of a clear, healthy koi pond.

4.4.2 Types of Algae

Understanding the different types of algae that commonly appear in koi ponds helps with managing them effectively:

Green Water Algae (Planktonic Algae)

- **Appearance:** This type of algae turns the pond water cloudy or pea-soup green. It consists of microscopic free-floating algae that bloom rapidly, especially in ponds with too much sunlight or excess nutrients.

- **Effects:** While koi can safely live in green water, the algae obstruct the view of the fish and lead to oxygen depletion at night.

String Algae (Filamentous Algae)

- **Appearance:** String algae form long, thread-like strands that grow on surfaces like rocks, waterfalls, and the sides of the pond. It's often found clinging to pond liners and can sometimes float to the surface in thick mats.

- **Effects:** String algae can clog filters and pumps, leading to reduced water flow and compromised equipment functionality. Additionally, thick growth can entangle koi, stressing or even trapping them.

4.4.3 Preventing Algae Blooms

Preventing algae overgrowth requires a combination of good pond management practices and the right tools. Here are some effective strategies:

1. Limit Sunlight Exposure

- **Why:** Algae thrive in sunlight, so reducing the amount of direct sun the pond receives can limit algae growth.

How

- Position the pond in a location that receives partial shade during the day, especially in the afternoon when the sun is strongest.
- Use floating plants like water lilies, lotus, and duckweed to provide natural shade. These plants cover the surface of the water, reducing light penetration and competing with algae for nutrients.
- For ponds in full sun, consider using pond covers or shade sails to block excessive sunlight during the hottest part of the day.

2. Reduce Nutrient Levels

- **Why:** Algae feed on nutrients such as nitrates and phosphates in the water. High nutrient levels lead to rapid algae blooms.

How

- Avoid overfeeding koi, as uneaten food breaks down and releases nutrients into the water.
- Perform regular water changes (10-20% weekly) to dilute excess nutrients and keep water chemistry balanced.
- Introduce aquatic plants that absorb nutrients, such as hornwort, anacharis, and water lettuce. These plants outcompete algae for the same nutrients, reducing its ability to thrive.
- Avoid using lawn fertilizers near the pond, as runoff can introduce phosphates and nitrates.

3. Introduce UV Sterilizers

- **Why:** UV sterilizers are effective in controlling green water algae by destroying free-floating algae cells.

How

- Install a UV clarifier in the pond's filtration system. As water passes through, the UV light kills algae cells, preventing them from reproducing and clearing up green water.
- UV sterilizers are most effective when used consistently but should be combined with other methods (such as plant shading) to achieve long-term results.

4. Use Algaecides and Natural Treatments

- **Why:** Chemical algaecides can be used as a last resort for severe algae problems but must be used carefully to avoid harming koi and beneficial bacteria.

How

- Choose a fish-safe algaecide if you need immediate results, but follow the instructions carefully to avoid overdosing. Be aware that dead algae can decompose quickly and reduce oxygen levels, so aeration is important after treatment.

- Natural treatments like barley straw extract are a gentler option. As the straw breaks down, it releases enzymes that help prevent algae growth. Barley straw products are available in extract form or in bundles that can be placed in the pond.

4.4.4 Common Pond Pests and How to Manage Them

Just as algae can disrupt the pond environment, pests can also become a nuisance. Some pests harm the fish, while others cause mechanical problems or detract from the overall pond ecosystem.

1. Snails

- **Role:** Certain species of snails can be beneficial to a pond by grazing on algae and cleaning surfaces. However, some snails reproduce rapidly and can overpopulate the pond, leading to clogged filters and competition for resources with koi.

Control Methods

- **Manual Removal:** Regularly check for snail populations and remove any excess snails by hand.
- **Predatory Fish:** Consider introducing fish species that eat snails, such as loaches or goldfish, to naturally control snail populations.

2. Mosquitoes

- **Role:** Mosquitoes are attracted to stagnant water and can lay eggs on the surface, leading to large mosquito populations around the pond.

Control Methods

- **Water Circulation:** Ensure good water movement by using aerators, fountains, or waterfalls. Mosquitoes cannot lay eggs in moving water.

- **Mosquito-Eating Fish:** Introduce fish species like guppies, mosquito fish, or minnows to the pond. These fish feed on mosquito larvae, helping to control the mosquito population naturally.

3. Herons and Other Predators

- **Role:** Herons, raccoons, cats, and other predators are attracted to koi ponds because they see the fish as an easy food source. Predators can stress the fish, cause injury, or even deplete the koi population.

Control Methods

- **Pond Netting:** Install netting over the pond to physically prevent predators from reaching the fish.

- **Motion-Activated Deterrents:** Use motion-activated sprinklers or lights to startle predators when they approach the pond.

- **Deeper Hiding Areas:** Create deep sections in the pond where koi can hide from predators. You can also add caves or rock structures for additional protection.

CHAPTER FIVE

CHOOSING HEALTHY KOI FISH

5.1 What to Look for When Buying Koi

Choosing healthy koi fish is crucial for ensuring the success and beauty of your pond. Healthy koi are more resilient, adapt better to new environments, and have the best chance of thriving in their new habitat. A koi that starts in good health will likely have a stronger immune system, vibrant colors, and better overall longevity. Starting with healthy fish also helps reduce the risk of introducing disease to your pond, protecting your entire koi population.

5.1.1 Sources for Buying Koi

When purchasing koi, the source is just as important as the fish itself. Here are the common places to buy koi:

- **Specialized Koi Breeders:** These breeders typically provide the highest quality fish with a focus on health and genetics. They can often provide valuable information on the koi's lineage, care instructions, and water conditions.

- **Fish Farms:** These are large-scale operations that offer a wide variety of koi sizes and colorations. While fish farms can be reputable, it's important to verify their health standards before purchasing.

- **Online Koi Stores:** Many online sellers ship koi fish directly to your door. When buying online, it's essential to check reviews, ensure the seller provides a live arrival guarantee, and that they are known for handling fish properly during transportation.

- **Local Pet Shops:** Local stores may carry koi, but the quality can vary widely. Ensure that the fish are housed in clean conditions and look healthy before making a purchase.

Regardless of where you purchase your koi, prioritize dealers who have a good reputation, practice proper fish care, and offer transparent health guarantees.

5.1.2 Visual Health Check

Before buying koi, it's essential to assess their overall health through visual inspection. Here's what to look for:

- **Body Shape:** Healthy koi have a smooth, symmetrical body shape. Avoid koi with deformities such as crooked spines, sunken bellies, or visible lumps, as these could be signs of genetic issues or malnourishment.

- **Skin Condition:** Check for smooth, blemish-free skin. The skin should be free of abrasions, sores, ulcers, or any visible parasites. Red, inflamed areas, or lesions could indicate bacterial infections or parasites that may spread to other fish.

- **Fins and Tail:** The fins and tail should be fully intact and without tears, fraying, or discoloration. Torn fins may be a sign of fin rot or injury, and clamped fins (fins held close to the body) may indicate stress or illness.

- **Coloration:** Koi are prized for their brilliant colors. Choose koi with bright, even coloring that aligns with the variety's natural characteristics. Faded or patchy colors could signal poor nutrition, stress, or illness. However, be wary of artificially color-enhanced koi, as these treatments can cause long-term health issues.

- **Eyes:** Clear, bright eyes are a good indicator of health. Cloudy or sunken eyes might be a sign of underlying illness or poor water conditions.

- **Swimming Behavior:** Observe how the koi move. Healthy koi will swim gracefully and confidently through the water, displaying curiosity and energy. Avoid fish that seem sluggish, hide excessively, or exhibit erratic swimming behavior, as these may be signs of illness or stress.

- **Breathing:** Normal breathing in koi should be steady and rhythmic. Fish that are gasping for air at the surface or have rapid, labored breathing may be experiencing water quality issues, gill problems, or other health concerns.

5.1.3 Avoiding Common Health Issues

While inspecting koi, be aware of the following common health concerns:

- **Parasites:** Koi can be prone to parasites like anchor worms, fish lice, and gill flukes. Symptoms of parasites include flashing (rubbing against objects), visible worms, or scales that appear irritated. Avoid buying koi from tanks where these issues are visible, as parasites can quickly spread to your pond.

- **Signs of Disease:** Some common koi diseases include bacterial infections, fungal growths, and viral diseases like Koi Herpes Virus (KHV). Symptoms to watch for include sores, white or cotton-like patches, clamped fins, and lethargy. Always avoid buying koi from environments where fish show signs of illness or poor care practices are evident.

5.1.4 Size and Age Considerations

Koi come in a variety of sizes, from small juvenile fish to fully-grown adults. When choosing koi, size and age play a role in care and cost:

- **Smaller/Younger Koi:** These fish are often more affordable and will grow over time. However, smaller koi may be more delicate and harder to evaluate for long-term health and coloration. Be prepared to provide them with ample space and proper nutrition to encourage healthy growth.

- **Larger/Older Koi:** Larger koi are more established in terms of size, coloration, and health. Their appearance will likely remain consistent, and it's easier to gauge their quality. However, they require more pond space, a higher volume of food, and more careful handling during transportation. Additionally, larger koi tend to be more expensive.

5.2 Transporting Koi Safely to Their New Home

5.2.1 Planning Ahead for Safe Transport

Proper planning is essential when transporting koi from a breeder, dealer, or pet store to your pond. Koi are sensitive creatures, especially during transportation when they are exposed to changes in water quality, temperature, and handling stress. A well-thought-out plan ensures the fish experience minimal stress, reducing the risk of injury or illness after they are introduced to their new environment.

Here are key steps to plan ahead for transporting koi:

- **Schedule the Trip in Advance:** Coordinate with the breeder or seller to choose the best time for pickup. This will allow you to plan the transportation when conditions are favorable.

- **Prepare the Pond:** Ensure the pond is ready for the new koi by checking the water parameters (e.g., temperature, pH, ammonia, nitrite levels) to match those of the transport water as closely as possible.

- **Transport Timing:** Choose a time when weather conditions are mild, preferably early morning or late evening, when temperatures are cooler. Avoid extreme weather days, especially if the journey will take a few hours or more.

5.2.2 Transport Bags and Containers

Koi are typically transported in specialized fish transport bags designed to keep the fish safe and comfortable during the trip. These bags are filled with oxygenated water and sealed securely to prevent leaks or water loss.

- **Koi Transport Bags:** These are large, durable plastic bags made for fish transport. When purchasing koi, ask the breeder or dealer to provide the proper transport bags. If you're transporting koi on your own, use a new, clean plastic bag to avoid contamination.

- **Bag Size and Water Volume:** Make sure the bag is large enough to provide ample water for the koi, with enough room for oxygen and movement. The general rule is to fill the bag only about one-third with water and leave two-thirds with air for the fish to breathe.

Double-Bagging for Safety

Double-bagging the koi is recommended to prevent leaks and protect the fish during transport. The outer bag provides an extra layer of security in case the inner bag punctures or leaks during transit.

- **How to Double-Bag:** Place the fish inside one bag, and then place that bag inside another for additional protection. Seal both bags tightly using rubber bands, ensuring no air or water can escape.

- **Bag Orientation:** Ensure that the bags remain upright throughout the trip, as flipping or tilting the bags can cause water to leak and stress the fish.

Oxygenation for Longer Trips

For journeys longer than an hour, oxygenated bags are critical. Koi require plenty of oxygen in the water, and standard air-filled bags may not provide enough for prolonged trips.

- **Oxygen Supply:** Breeders and koi dealers typically have access to oxygen tanks, which they use to fill transport bags with pure oxygen. This prolongs the oxygen supply in the water and keeps the fish healthy for longer trips.

- **Portable Oxygen Systems:** For those transporting koi frequently or over long distances, investing in a small portable oxygen tank system can be beneficial.

Temperature Control During Transport

Temperature stability is vital for the health of koi. Rapid fluctuations can cause shock or stress, potentially leading to illness. During transport, take measures to keep the water temperature consistent.

- **Optimal Transport Temperature:** Ideally, transport koi in water that matches the pond temperature or within a small temperature range (no more than a few degrees' difference).
- **Transport Time of Day:** As previously mentioned, early morning or late evening transport is preferable to avoid the heat of the day.

This prevents sudden spikes in temperature while on the road.

Using Insulated Containers

Insulated containers, such as coolers or Styrofoam boxes, provide excellent temperature control during koi transport. Placing the transport bags inside an insulated container helps shield the fish from direct sunlight and temperature fluctuations caused by wind or drafts.

- **Cooler Sizes:** Choose a cooler that is large enough to hold the transport bags securely but small enough to maintain stable temperatures. For short trips, a small cooler may be sufficient, but for longer journeys, a larger, well-insulated cooler is ideal.

- **Extra Protection:** If transporting during very hot or cold weather, consider adding ice packs or heat packs to the cooler. However, make sure these do not come into direct contact with the transport bag to avoid sudden extreme temperature changes.

Avoiding Long Delays

Minimizing the time koi spend in transport is crucial to reducing stress. Prolonged transportation exposes the fish to confined spaces, limited oxygen, and fluctuating temperatures, all of which can be harmful.

- **Efficient Travel Route:** Plan the most direct route to your destination, avoiding unnecessary stops or detours. If traveling a long distance, consider taking breaks to check on the koi's condition and ensure the bags are stable.

- **Travel Time:** Aim to keep the travel time under two hours if possible. For longer trips, you may need to make additional preparations such as adding more oxygen, ensuring temperature control, and monitoring the fish periodically.

Transporting Multiple Fish

When transporting multiple koi, it's important to ensure that each fish has enough space to avoid overcrowding, which can lead to injuries or stress.

- **One Fish per Bag:** For larger koi, each fish should be transported in its own bag to avoid any damage caused by rubbing against one another during the trip. This also ensures that each fish has enough oxygen and water.

- **Small Koi:** Smaller or juvenile koi may be transported together in larger bags, but care should be taken to avoid overcrowding. A good rule of thumb is to have no more than 2-3 small koi in one large bag, ensuring that they still have enough space and oxygen.

- **Transporting Multiple Bags:** When transporting several bags, ensure that they are securely placed inside the vehicle. Avoid stacking bags on top of each other to prevent damage or leaks.

5.2.3 Arrival at the Pond: The Acclimation Process

Once you arrive at your destination, don't immediately release the koi into the pond. Acclimating the fish to the pond's temperature and water parameters is essential to avoid shock.

- **Float the Bag:** Place the sealed transport bag in the pond for 15-20 minutes. This allows the water temperature in the bag to gradually adjust to the pond's temperature.

- **Introduce Pond Water:** After the bag has floated, gradually introduce small amounts of pond water into the transport bag. Repeat this process every 5-10 minutes for about 30 minutes. This helps the koi adjust to the new water chemistry.

- **Release the Koi:** Once the water temperature and chemistry have stabilized, gently release the koi into the pond. Let the fish swim out on its own to minimize stress.

5.3 Quarantine Procedures for New Koi

5.3.1 Why Quarantine is Crucial

Introducing new koi to your pond without proper quarantine can pose significant risks to the health of your existing fish. New koi, even from reputable breeders, can carry diseases, parasites, or bacteria that may not be immediately visible. Quarantining new fish acts as a precautionary measure, giving you time to monitor their health and treat any potential problems before they come into contact with your established koi population. This procedure can save you from potential outbreaks of serious conditions like Koi Herpes Virus (KHV), parasitic infestations, and bacterial infections.

Length of Quarantine

The recommended quarantine period for new koi is 2 to 4 weeks. During this time, it is essential to observe the new koi closely for any signs of disease or stress. This period allows potential pathogens or parasites to become apparent before introducing the fish to the main pond. In some cases, if there are any signs of illness, the quarantine period may need to be extended until the fish are completely healthy.

5.3.2 Quarantine Tank Setup
Setting up a proper quarantine tank is key to ensuring the health and well-being of your koi during this observation period.

- **Size and Water Volume:** The quarantine tank should be large enough to comfortably house the new koi. A tank of at least 100 gallons is recommended for smaller koi, with larger tanks needed for larger or multiple fish. The tank should provide enough space for the koi to swim and move around freely to reduce stress. Overcrowding in the quarantine tank can increase stress and the risk of illness.

- **Filtration and Aeration:** Proper filtration is critical to maintaining clean water and optimal health conditions in the quarantine tank. Use a reliable filtration system to handle waste and keep the water free of ammonia and nitrite buildup, which can harm the koi. Aeration is also essential, as koi require oxygen-rich water to remain healthy. Ensure there is enough aeration through air stones or a good water flow to maintain adequate oxygen levels.

- **Water Temperature:** The temperature of the quarantine tank should closely match that of the main pond to prevent temperature shock when the koi are eventually moved. A consistent temperature of around 65°F to 75°F is ideal for koi health. You can use a heater or chiller to maintain the temperature, and it's important to gradually adjust the temperature before transferring the koi to avoid shock.

- **Shelter and Shade:** Providing the koi with places to hide during quarantine helps reduce stress. You can add PVC pipes, plastic crates, or other types of shelter that allow the koi to retreat when they feel threatened. Stress reduction is crucial during quarantine to prevent illness and aid recovery if needed.

5.3.3 Monitoring Health During Quarantine

Closely monitoring the health of the koi during quarantine is a fundamental part of the process. Regular observation helps you catch potential issues early, allowing you to take action before introducing the fish to the main pond.

- **Daily Observation:** Check your koi daily for any signs of disease or abnormal behavior. Key signs to watch for include:
- Loss of appetite
- Erratic swimming patterns (such as darting or circling)
- Flashing (scratching against objects)
- Visible lesions, ulcers, or sores on the skin
- Clamped fins or skin discoloration
- Lethargy or remaining at the bottom of the tank
- **Water Testing:** Maintaining high water quality in the quarantine tank is crucial. Test the water frequently to ensure the levels of pH, ammonia, nitrite, and nitrate remain within safe limits. Sudden spikes in toxins like ammonia can stress the koi and weaken their immune system, making them more susceptible to disease.

- **Parasite Control:** New koi often carry external parasites, which can spread quickly if not managed. Salt dips or medicated baths are a common preventative treatment to eliminate external parasites like gill flukes or anchor worms. Consult with a koi veterinarian or expert before administering any medications, as incorrect dosing can harm your fish.

- **Bacterial Infections:** Be on the lookout for bacterial infections, which can manifest as ulcers, redness, or frayed fins. These infections may require antibiotic treatments, depending on the severity. If you spot any signs of bacterial issues, consult a veterinarian specializing in koi for appropriate treatment advice.

5.3.4 Acclimating Koi to the Main Pond

Once the quarantine period is over and the koi show no signs of illness or distress, it's time to acclimate them to the main pond. However, this should be done gradually to prevent shock and ensure a smooth transition.

- **Gradual Acclimation:** The koi should be acclimated to the water temperature and chemistry of the main pond slowly. Start by placing the koi in their transport bag (or bucket) and floating it in the pond for 15-30 minutes. This allows the temperature in the bag to slowly match the pond water.

- **Slow Introduction of Pond Water:** After floating the bag, gradually introduce small amounts of pond water into the transport bag. Adding pond water in small increments over 15-20 minutes helps the koi adjust to the pond's specific water chemistry (pH, hardness, etc.). This is particularly important if there are significant differences between the quarantine tank water and the pond water.

- **Releasing the Koi:** Once the water temperature and chemistry have been equalized, gently release the koi into the pond. Let the koi swim out on their own, avoiding any sudden movements that might stress the fish. If using a bucket, tilt it slowly into the pond to allow the fish to swim out freely.

Best Practices for Quarantining Koi

- **Dedicated Equipment:** Use separate nets, buckets, and siphons for the quarantine tank to avoid cross-contamination with the main pond.
- **Regular Water Changes:** Perform weekly water changes of about 10-20% to maintain water quality in the quarantine tank. Use dechlorinated water to avoid any harmful chemical exposure.

- **Lighting:** Keep lighting in the quarantine tank subdued to help reduce stress on the koi during this adjustment period.

CHAPTER SIX

FEEDING YOUR KOI

6.1 Koi Diet and Nutritional Needs

Koi are omnivorous fish, meaning they consume a wide variety of both plant and animal matter in their natural environment. In the wild, koi forage for algae, small insects, larvae, and plant material, which provides them with a diverse range of nutrients essential for their health and development. In a pond environment, it is important to replicate this diverse diet as closely as possible to ensure they get the right balance of nutrients for optimal growth, energy, immune function, and vibrant coloration. A well-rounded diet will enhance their longevity and overall well-being.

6.1.1 Essential Nutrients for Koi

To provide the best possible nutrition, koi need a combination of proteins, carbohydrates, fats, vitamins, minerals, and fiber. Each of these nutrients plays a specific role in maintaining their health.

1. Proteins

Proteins are one of the most critical nutrients in a koi's diet, particularly for younger koi (fry and juveniles) that are still growing. Protein is essential for muscle development, tissue repair, and growth. Koi food should contain high-quality protein sources, such as fish meal, shrimp meal, or soy protein, to support these processes. For younger koi, the protein content in food should be higher (typically around 35-40%), while adult koi require slightly less, around 30-35%.

- **Importance for Growth:** Adequate protein intake helps koi achieve proper size and muscle strength.

- **Best Sources:** Look for koi foods that list fish meal, shrimp meal, or other marine-based proteins as primary ingredients, as these provide easily digestible and bioavailable protein.

2. Carbohydrates

Carbohydrates are primarily used by koi as a source of energy, allowing them to remain active and maintain their metabolic processes. However, koi are less efficient at metabolizing carbohydrates compared to other animals, meaning they do not require large amounts in their diet. Overfeeding carbohydrates can lead to poor water quality as the koi are unable to utilize them efficiently, causing the excess nutrients to pollute the water.

- **Moderation is Key:** Carbohydrates should make up 20-30% of a koi's diet, and they should come from natural, whole-food sources like wheat germ or rice rather than processed fillers.

- **Potential Issues:** Excess carbohydrates can contribute to fat buildup and poor water quality due to undigested material breaking down in the pond.

3. Fats

Fats serve as a concentrated source of energy for koi and are particularly important during times of increased activity, growth, or colder weather when koi require extra energy to maintain body temperature. Fats also support the absorption of fat-soluble vitamins (A, D, E, and K) and help maintain healthy skin, scales, and immune function.

- **Energy Source:** Fats help koi store energy and maintain reserves for periods when food might be less abundant or water temperatures drop.

- **Cold Weather Needs:** Koi tend to eat less during the colder months, but their bodies rely on fat stores for energy to sustain them when their metabolism slows down.

- **Fat Content:** A diet containing around 5-10% fat is typically sufficient for koi, with some seasonal variation to account for colder months.

4. Vitamins and Minerals

Vitamins and minerals are essential for various bodily functions in koi, including immune support, bone strength, and metabolic regulation.

- **Vitamin C:** One of the most important vitamins for koi, vitamin C boosts their immune system and aids in the repair of damaged tissues. It also plays a role in collagen production, which is important for maintaining healthy skin, fins, and scales. Without adequate vitamin C, koi can develop bone deformities and weakened immune systems.

- **Minerals:** Koi require calcium and phosphorus to maintain strong bones and scales. Minerals also play a crucial role in enzyme functions and other metabolic processes. Minerals like potassium and sodium help in maintaining osmotic balance, ensuring that koi can regulate water intake and maintain hydration.

- **Supplementing Vitamins and Minerals:** A high-quality koi food will include the necessary vitamins and minerals. You can also occasionally offer fresh vegetables (like lettuce or spinach) or fruits to provide additional nutrients.

5. Fiber

Though often overlooked, fiber plays a significant role in maintaining koi's digestive health. Fiber helps prevent digestive blockages and ensures that koi process their food efficiently.

- **Supporting Digestion:** The right amount of fiber ensures that koi avoid digestive issues like constipation, which can be a problem in pond environments if their diet is too low in roughage.

- **Sources of Fiber:** Plant matter such as algae, vegetables, and some grains offer fiber that keeps koi digestion in check. Avoid overfeeding koi with fibrous food, though, as excessive fiber can result in nutrient loss.

6.1.2 Balancing the Diet

Maintaining a balanced diet for koi is essential for their long-term health. While koi can survive on basic pellet foods, a diet rich in variety provides the most benefits, enhancing their natural coloration and vitality.

- **Pellet Foods:** High-quality koi pellets should form the staple diet, offering the correct balance of proteins, fats, carbohydrates, vitamins, and minerals. Opt for pellets that are free from artificial fillers like corn or soy, which can reduce water quality and provide little nutritional value to koi.

- **Fresh Foods:** Supplementing their diet with fresh foods like vegetables (lettuce, spinach, peas) and live foods (earthworms, shrimp) ensures koi receive all the necessary nutrients while adding variety to their meals.

- **Feeding by Developmental Stage:** Adjust the diet depending on the koi's life stage. Fry need a protein-rich diet to support rapid growth, while adult koi require a more balanced diet with slightly lower protein content. During spawning or cold months, you can adjust the diet to include more fat and nutrients to support koi through these different conditions.

6.1.3 Seasonal Feeding

It's also important to adjust feeding practices based on the seasons:

- **Spring and Summer:** During warmer months, koi are more active, and their metabolism is faster. Feed higher-protein diets to support growth and development.

- **Autumn:** As temperatures drop, begin feeding koi more carbohydrates and fats to help them build reserves for the winter.

- **Winter:** In winter, koi's metabolism slows, and they require little food. Use a low-protein, high-fat diet or stop feeding altogether if the water temperature drops below 50°F (10°C).

6.2 Choosing the Right Food for Growth and Color Enhancement

Feeding koi is more than just providing them with nutrition—it plays a significant role in their overall development and appearance. Selecting the right type of food is crucial for promoting growth, enhancing color, and maintaining their health. Understanding the various food types and their specific benefits will allow you to tailor the diet for optimal results, especially if you're aiming for larger, more colorful koi.

6.2.1 Types of Koi Food

The variety of koi food on the market can seem overwhelming, but it breaks down into several categories, each with its own pros and cons. Here's an overview of the most common types:

1. Pellets

Pellets are the most widely available and commonly used koi food, primarily because they are formulated to meet koi's nutritional needs and come in different sizes to suit various life stages.

- **Pellet Sizes:** Choosing the right pellet size is important for both digestion and feeding efficiency.

- **Small Pellets (1-2mm):** These are ideal for younger or smaller koi, as they are easier for them to swallow and digest.

- **Medium Pellets (3-5mm):** Suitable for koi in the juvenile stage, medium-sized pellets provide balanced nutrition without being difficult to consume.

- **Large Pellets (6-8mm):** These are for adult or larger koi, helping to prevent them from gulping down too much air, which can cause buoyancy issues.

Floating vs. Sinking Pellets

Floating pellets allow you to observe your koi's eating behavior and ensure that each fish is getting enough food. However, some koi may be more inclined to feed at lower levels in the pond. Sinking pellets are better for koi that prefer feeding from the bottom, but they require you to monitor water quality closely, as uneaten food can spoil if left unattended.

2. Flakes

Flakes are less common but still available for feeding smaller koi. Flakes are often more prone to breaking down in water, which can affect water quality and cause filtration issues. While they are a viable option for small or young koi, they are not ideal for long-term use due to their tendency to dissolve quickly.

- **Suitable for Small Koi:** Flakes can be used for fry or young koi that have trouble eating pellets, but they should be phased out as the koi grow.

3. Sticks

Floating sticks are another option that many koi keepers use. Like pellets, they come in different sizes and contain essential nutrients. Because they float, sticks make it easier to observe koi while they feed, ensuring that all fish are receiving food evenly.

- **Ease of Monitoring:** Floating sticks are convenient for koi owners who want to monitor feeding behavior and check for signs of illness or disinterest in food.
- **Larger Koi:** Sticks are especially useful for larger koi, as they tend to stay at the water's surface, making them easy to access.

4. Freeze-Dried and Frozen Foods

These are high-protein supplements that should be used as part of a varied diet. Freeze-dried or frozen options like bloodworms, krill, brine shrimp, and tubifex worms provide an excellent source of protein and mimic koi's natural diet in the wild. These foods should be given as occasional treats rather than staples.

- **Benefits:** These foods provide important nutrients like amino acids and can help promote muscle development and growth.
- **Considerations:** Since they are richer and more calorically dense than regular pellets, they should not be overfed to prevent koi from becoming overweight or having digestive issues.

6. Live Foods

Live foods such as earthworms, mosquito larvae, and daphnia offer an excellent way to provide natural, nutrient-dense meals for koi while encouraging their natural foraging behavior. However, live foods carry a risk of parasites or disease if not sourced from a reliable supplier.

- **Nutrient-Rich:** Live foods are great for stimulating growth and enhancing activity levels in koi.

- **Potential Risks:** Live foods must be sourced carefully to avoid introducing pathogens or parasites into the pond. Consider raising your own live food cultures or purchasing from trusted suppliers.

7. Growth-Enhancing Food

Certain koi foods are specifically formulated to promote rapid growth, particularly in younger fish. These foods contain high levels of protein, often in the form of fish meal or shrimp meal, and are packed with essential amino acids that are critical for building tissue and muscle.

- **High-Protein Formulas:** Growth-enhancing koi foods often contain 35-45% protein, significantly higher than maintenance foods for adult koi. These are ideal for juvenile koi or during the summer months when koi are most active and their metabolism is at its peak.

- **Caution with Overfeeding:** Overfeeding growth food can cause koi to grow too quickly, leading to potential deformities or weakened immune systems. It is important to balance their diet and avoid feeding growth food exclusively.

- **When to Use:** Feed growth-enhancing food during warmer months when koi are active, as their bodies can efficiently process the extra nutrients.

6.2.2 Color-Enhancing Food

Koi are prized for their vibrant colors, and specialized koi foods can help enhance and intensify these hues, particularly the reds, oranges, and yellows. Color-enhancing foods contain natural pigments such as astaxanthin, spirulina, and carotenoids, which help amplify the koi's natural coloration

- **Astaxanthin:** A red-orange pigment found in krill and shrimp, astaxanthin enhances red and orange colors in koi. It is a powerful antioxidant and beneficial to koi health.

- **Spirulina:** This blue-green alga is rich in protein and pigments, helping to brighten whites and intensify blues and greens. Spirulina also supports immune health and digestion.

- **Carotenoids:** Naturally occurring pigments that contribute to the vibrant reds, oranges, and yellows in koi. These are found in ingredients like shrimp meal, krill, and other seafood-based products.

- **How It Works:** Pigments are absorbed by the koi and deposited in their skin, enhancing the vibrancy of their colors. However, they do not create new colors, only amplify what is already present in the fish's genetic makeup.

- **Supplementing vs. Regular Use:** Color-enhancing food can be part of the regular diet, but should be used in moderation. Overuse can result in color saturation, where reds become overly intense, potentially overpowering other colors like white or blue.

6.2.3 Balancing Color Food

While color-enhancing food can greatly improve the appearance of your koi, it is important to balance it with a staple diet that meets all nutritional needs. Excessive use of color food can sometimes lead to color imbalances, where one color becomes overly dominant, and the koi's natural beauty may be compromised.

- **Moderation is Key:** Introduce color-enhancing food gradually, using it as a supplement to the koi's staple food. This ensures that the koi's diet remains nutritionally balanced while still enhancing their natural pigmentation.

- **Rotating Diets:** Rotate between growth, maintenance, and color-enhancing foods depending on the koi's seasonal needs, size, and age. This helps avoid overfeeding specific nutrients and ensures that your koi receive a comprehensive diet year-round.

6.3 How Often and How Much to Feed Koi

Feeding koi properly is crucial for maintaining their health, growth, and overall well-being. Factors such as age, water temperature, and seasonal changes significantly affect koi's feeding habits and nutritional needs. Understanding how often and how much to feed your koi will help prevent overfeeding, promote healthy growth, and maintain good water quality in your pond.

6.3.1 Feeding Frequency

Koi feeding frequency depends on a combination of factors, including their age, the season, and the water temperature. Here's a guide to feeding koi based on these conditions:

1. Young Koi

- **Feeding Schedule:** Young koi (also known as fry or juvenile koi) are growing rapidly and have higher metabolic demands. During the warmer months (when water temperatures are between 65°F and 80°F / 18°C and 27°C), young koi should be fed 3-4 times a day. At this stage, they require high-protein foods to support muscle development and growth. Frequent feedings ensure they get enough nutrition for proper development without overwhelming the pond's filtration system.

- **Special Considerations:** It's important to use small-sized pellets or specialized fry food to ensure the young koi can easily consume their meals.

2. Adult Koi

- **Feeding Schedule:** Adult koi, who have reached a stable growth phase, do not need to eat as often as younger koi. In warm weather, adult koi can be fed 1-2 times a day. Feeding them more frequently can lead to overconsumption, which increases waste production and puts stress on the pond's filtration system. In general, feed adult koi once in the morning and, if necessary, again in the early evening, when they are still active and the water is warmest.

- **Balance and Variety:** While adult koi don't need as much protein as young koi, they still benefit from a balanced diet that includes a mix of pellets, vegetables, and protein-based treats.

3. Cold Weather Feeding

- **Metabolism and Temperature:** As water temperatures drop below 50°F (10°C), koi's metabolism slows significantly. During these colder months (usually fall and winter), koi enter a state of semi-hibernation, reducing their energy requirements and digestion speed.

- **Below 50°F:** When water temperatures fall below 50°F (10°C), it's recommended to stop feeding koi altogether, as they cannot properly digest food in cold water. Feeding during this time can lead to undigested food sitting in their stomachs, which may cause illness or death.

- **50°F to 60°F (10°C to 16°C):** In this range, reduce feeding to once every 2-3 days and switch to a low-protein, wheat germ-based diet that is easier for koi to digest in cooler water.

Resuming Feeding: Once water temperatures rise again in spring, you can gradually resume normal feeding routines, slowly increasing the frequency as temperatures rise.

6.3.2 Portion Control

Portion control is as critical as feeding frequency. Overfeeding is one of the most common mistakes in koi care and can lead to serious problems such as poor water quality, ammonia buildup, and fish obesity. Koi do not have a natural off-switch when it comes to eating, so they will continue eating even when full, leading to excess waste production and increased strain on the pond's filtration system.

1. General Rule

- A commonly recommended guideline is to feed koi only as much food as they can consume within 5 minutes. After five minutes, any leftover food should be promptly removed from the pond to prevent it from sinking, decomposing, and contaminating the water.

- **Why 5 Minutes?** This timeframe allows koi to consume food efficiently without the risk of excess waste settling in the pond. Removing uneaten food also helps avoid spikes in ammonia levels that could be harmful to the fish.

2. Adjusting Portions

- **Seasonal Adjustments:** During the summer, when koi are most active, they may require slightly more food to match their increased energy needs. Conversely, in cooler months, feed less to match their reduced metabolism.

- **Water Quality and Filtration:** Ponds with excellent filtration systems may support slightly larger feedings without a significant impact on water quality. However, in ponds with minimal filtration or smaller water volumes, overfeeding can quickly lead to poor water conditions and algae growth.

Koi Size and Age

- Larger Koi need more food, but the quantity should still be controlled to avoid overfeeding. You can break up their total daily food intake into smaller, more frequent feedings.
- Smaller Koi may require smaller, more frequent meals to aid in their growth and development.

3. Signs of Overfeeding

- **Cloudy or Green Water:** Overfeeding can result in water cloudiness or algae growth, as uneaten food and waste increase nutrient levels in the water, leading to algae blooms.

- **Floating Food:** If food is left floating after five minutes, you are likely overfeeding. Reduce the portion size and remove any uneaten food promptly.

- **Ammonia Spikes:** Test the pond's water regularly for ammonia levels. Elevated ammonia levels are a direct consequence of excess fish waste, often caused by overfeeding.

6.3.3 Adjusting for Koi Size and Pond Conditions

Feeding requirements also depend on the size of the koi and the conditions of the pond. Here's how to adjust based on these factors:

1. Size of Koi

- **Growing Koi:** Koi in a growth phase (typically younger koi) require more frequent and larger amounts of protein-rich food to support their development. Keep in mind that this should be balanced with good water quality management.

- **Mature Koi:** For older, mature koi that are not growing as rapidly, feeding 1-2 times per day with smaller portions will prevent overeating and maintain stable pond conditions.

2. Pond Size and Stocking Density

- **Larger Ponds:** Koi in larger ponds with more room to swim and grow may need slightly more food because they are more active and can spread out the waste. These ponds often have better natural filtration and larger surface areas for beneficial bacteria to break down waste.

- **Smaller or Heavily Stocked Ponds:** If your pond is smaller or heavily stocked with many koi, there is a greater risk of waste buildup and water quality issues. In these cases, err on the side of feeding less to reduce nutrient levels and avoid overwhelming the filtration system.

3. Water Conditions

- **Filtration:** In ponds with excellent filtration systems, koi can be fed slightly larger portions without major impacts on water quality. However, in ponds with minimal filtration, keep feeding amounts low to avoid rapid water degradation.

- **Water Temperature:** Koi's metabolism is directly tied to water temperature. In warmer water, koi will be more active and metabolize food faster, so you can feed more frequently. In colder water, reduce feeding or stop altogether, as koi cannot digest food as efficiently.

CHAPTER SEVEN

KEEPING YOUR KOI HEALTHY

7.1 Common Koi Health Issues and How to Prevent Them

7.1.1 Common Koi Health Issues and How to Prevent Them

Koi are hardy and resilient fish, but they are still vulnerable to various health issues, especially when their environment or care is compromised. Common health problems in koi are often related to poor water quality, stress, overcrowding, or the introduction of new fish without proper quarantine. Prevention and early detection are crucial in maintaining a healthy pond and ensuring your koi thrive.

1. Parasites

Parasites are one of the most common health threats to koi, and they can cause significant damage if left untreated. They often irritate the skin, gills, and fins, leading to secondary infections.

Common Parasites

- Flukes (gill and body flukes) are small flatworms that attach to the koi's skin or gills, causing irritation, weight loss, and lethargy.
- Anchor Worms (Lernaea) are crustacean parasites that burrow into the skin, leaving behind ulcers and open wounds.
- Fish Lice (Argulus) are visible to the naked eye and attach themselves to the koi, causing irritation and inflammation.

Symptoms

- Scratching against objects
- Lethargy
- Red or irritated skin
- Weight loss

- Flashing behavior (rapid movement where koi brush their sides against surfaces)

Prevention

- **Regular Pond Maintenance:** Clean water is essential in reducing the likelihood of parasitic infestations. Ensure the pond filter is functioning properly and remove debris regularly.

- **Quarantine Procedures:** Always quarantine new fish for at least 2-4 weeks before introducing them to the main pond. This reduces the chance of parasites spreading to your existing koi.

- **UV Sterilizers:** Some koi keepers use UV sterilizers, which help kill free-floating parasites and their larvae by exposing them to ultraviolet light. These devices can reduce the overall parasite load in the water.

2. Fungal Infections

Fungal infections often affect koi that are already weakened by other health issues, such as injuries, parasites, or poor water quality. Fungi typically invade open wounds or stressed fish, leading to unsightly growths and potentially fatal infections if untreated.

Symptoms

- White, cotton-like growths on the skin, fins, or gills.

- Ulceration around the infected area.

- Lethargy or lack of appetite.

Prevention

- **Water Quality:** Maintain excellent water quality through regular water changes, proper filtration, and monitoring parameters such as pH, ammonia, nitrite, and nitrate levels.

- **Strong Immune System:** A well-balanced diet and stress-free environment will help keep your koi's immune system strong, making them more resistant to fungal infections.

- **Injury Treatment:** Promptly treat any injuries your koi may have. Open wounds are an entry point for fungi, so applying a topical antiseptic or healing solution can prevent fungal growth.

- **Salt Treatments:** Some koi keepers use salt baths to treat mild fungal infections, as salt can inhibit fungal spores and support healing. However, this should only be used in moderation and under expert guidance.

3. Bacterial Infections

Bacterial diseases are common in koi and often result from poor water quality, overcrowding, or injury. These infections can range from external issues like ulcers to internal problems such as septicemia.

Common Bacterial Diseases

- **Ulcers:** Open sores on the skin caused by opportunistic bacteria. These can become deep and infected if not treated promptly.
- **Fin Rot:** A condition where the fins and tail appear ragged and frayed, caused by bacterial infection.
- **Columnaris:** A bacterial disease that leads to lesions on the gills, mouth, and fins. It often spreads rapidly in warm water.

Symptoms

- Red sores or ulcers on the body.
- Fraying or discoloration of the fins.
- Lethargy or labored breathing.
- Swelling or bloating.

Prevention

- **Clean Water:** Regular water changes and a well-maintained filtration system are essential in preventing bacterial outbreaks. Dirty water promotes bacterial growth and weakens the fish's immune system.

- **Water Testing:** Regularly test the water for key parameters like ammonia, nitrite, and nitrate levels. Keeping these at safe levels will reduce the stress on your koi and their susceptibility to infections.

- **Avoid Overcrowding:** An overcrowded pond can increase stress and lower oxygen levels, making koi more vulnerable to bacterial diseases.

- **Quarantine New Fish:** Isolating new koi for a minimum of 30 days before introducing them to the pond can prevent the introduction of new bacteria into the system.

4. Swim Bladder Issues

The swim bladder is an organ that helps koi control their buoyancy and maintain balance. Swim bladder problems can occur due to various factors, including poor diet, infection, or injury.

Symptoms

- Difficulty swimming or maintaining balance.
- Floating to the surface uncontrollably or sinking to the bottom.
- Tilting to one side or struggling to remain upright.

Prevention

- **Balanced Diet:** Overfeeding or feeding low-quality food high in carbohydrates can cause digestive blockages that affect the swim bladder. Feeding a balanced, varied diet with high-quality koi food will help prevent such issues.
- **Avoid Overfeeding:** Koi can be prone to digestive problems if they eat too much or too quickly. Feed them small amounts that they can consume within 5 minutes.

- **Soak Dry Food:** Some koi keepers pre-soak pellet food to reduce the risk of the fish swallowing air, which can lead to buoyancy problems.

- **Maintain Water Quality:** Poor water quality can also lead to stress and infection, which can in turn affect the swim bladder. Regular water changes and filtration are essential.

5. Koi Herpes Virus (KHV)

Koi Herpes Virus (KHV) is a highly contagious and often fatal virus that primarily affects koi and carp. It can cause mass die-offs in koi ponds if not detected and managed quickly.

Symptoms

Severe gill necrosis (gill tissue death), leading to difficulty breathing.

- Lethargy and loss of appetite.
- Sunken eyes and pale skin.

- Rapid and widespread mortality within the pond.

Prevention

- **Quarantine New Koi:** Quarantine any new koi for at least 30 days before adding them to your main pond. This can help prevent the introduction of KHV to your established population.

- **Maintain Pond Hygiene:** Keep the pond clean, reduce stress factors such as overcrowding and poor water quality, and monitor water temperature (KHV thrives in warmer water above 70°F / 21°C).

- **Stress Reduction:** Reducing stress through proper pond management and nutrition strengthens koi's immune system, making them less susceptible to viruses like KHV.

- **Vaccination:** In some regions, vaccines may be available to prevent KHV outbreaks, although they are not always 100% effective.

- **No Cure:** Unfortunately, there is no cure for KHV, and once infected, koi either die or remain carriers of the virus for life. The best defense is prevention through strict quarantine measures and proper pond management.

7.2 Recognizing Symptoms of Disease

Early detection of health problems in koi is vital for timely intervention and treatment. Koi are generally hardy, but if they fall ill, subtle changes in their behavior, appearance, or activity can be the first clues to an underlying issue. Understanding the symptoms of common diseases and stress-related conditions allows you to take prompt action and prevent serious health problems from escalating.

1. Changes in Appetite

One of the most noticeable early signs of illness is a change in eating habits. Koi are typically active feeders, especially during warmer months when their metabolism is high.

Symptoms

- Sudden loss of appetite or refusal to eat.
- Reduced interest in food that they normally enjoy.
- Only eating smaller amounts despite appearing otherwise healthy.

Potential Causes

- **Water Quality Issues:** High levels of ammonia, nitrites, or nitrates can cause stress and reduce appetite.
- **Illness:** Bacterial, fungal, or parasitic infections often cause koi to stop eating as they focus energy on fighting off the disease.
- **Temperature Changes:** As water temperature drops, koi naturally eat less, but a sudden drop in appetite during warm months may indicate illness.

2. Lethargy or Erratic Swimming

Healthy koi are typically curious, active, and alert, moving gracefully through the water. Any significant deviation from their usual activity level can be a red flag.

Symptoms

- **Lethargy:** Koi spending excessive time resting at the bottom of the pond or remaining motionless near the surface.

- **Erratic Swimming:** Uncoordinated swimming, darting around, or struggling to maintain balance or buoyancy.

Potential Causes

- **Stress:** Poor water quality, overcrowding, or drastic changes in water temperature can cause koi to become lethargic.

- **Swim Bladder Issues:** Erratic or unbalanced swimming may indicate swim bladder dysfunction caused by overfeeding or digestive problems.

- **Infections:** Bacterial, parasitic, or fungal infections can cause physical weakness, leading to lethargy or abnormal swimming patterns.

3. Visible Sores, Ulcers, or Bumps

Physical abnormalities on a koi's body are clear signs that something is wrong. These can range from small sores to more serious ulcers or growths.

Symptoms

- **Sores or Lesions:** Open wounds or patches of discolored, inflamed skin.

- **Ulcers:** Deep, open wounds that can result from bacterial infections.

- **Bumps:** Raised lumps on the body or fins, which may indicate parasitic infestations or viral infections.

Potential Causes

- **Bacterial Infections:** Ulcers and sores are often caused by bacterial infections, particularly when koi are stressed by poor water quality.
- **Parasites:** Anchor worms, flukes, and other parasites can cause skin damage, leading to sores or bumps.
- **Physical Injury:** Koi may injure themselves on sharp objects in the pond, which can become infected if not treated promptly.

4. Gasping at the Surface

Koi often come to the surface to feed, but if they seem to be gasping for air more frequently or for extended periods, it could be a sign of a serious issue, particularly related to oxygen levels or gill health.

Symptoms

- Koi continuously swimming near the surface, opening and closing their mouths.
- Appearing to gulp for air at the water's surface.

Potential Causes

- **Low Oxygen Levels:** Warm water holds less dissolved oxygen, and koi may gasp at the surface if oxygen levels in the pond are too low.
- **Gill Damage:** Parasitic infections, such as gill flukes, or bacterial infections can damage the gills, making it harder for koi to absorb oxygen.
- **Overcrowding:** Too many fish in a small pond can deplete oxygen levels, especially if the pond lacks adequate filtration or aeration.

5. Discoloration or Red Streaks

Healthy koi are known for their vibrant colors. A sudden change in coloration, particularly red streaks in the fins or along the body, often indicates stress or disease.

Symptoms

- Fading or dulling of the koi's natural colors.
- Bright red streaks or blotches on the body or fins, usually indicating irritation or internal bleeding.

Potential Causes

- **Poor Water Quality:** High levels of toxins like ammonia or nitrites can cause stress, leading to discoloration or red streaks in the fins.
- **Infections:** Bacterial or parasitic infections can result in visible inflammation and red patches.
- **Stress:** Environmental stressors, such as fluctuating water temperatures or overcrowding,

may cause a change in coloration or red streaks as the koi's body reacts to the stress.

6. Flashing or Scratching

Flashing refers to a koi rubbing or scraping its body against objects in the pond, such as rocks, plants, or the sides of the pond. This behavior is usually a sign of irritation.

Symptoms

- Koi repeatedly rubbing themselves against pond surfaces.

- Erratic, sudden movements followed by flashing behavior.

Potential Causes

- **Parasites:** Flashing is often caused by external parasites like flukes, anchor worms, or fish lice. The irritation leads the koi to try to relieve the itching by scraping themselves against objects.

- **Skin Infections:** Fungal or bacterial infections can cause skin irritation, leading to flashing behavior.
- **Poor Water Quality:** High levels of toxins or irritants in the water can make koi uncomfortable, causing them to scratch their skin.

7. Clamped Fins

A koi's fins should normally be open and extended when swimming. Clamped fins, where the fins are held close to the body, are a common sign of stress or illness.

Symptoms

- Fins are consistently pressed tightly against the body rather than spread out while swimming.
- Reduced movement or stiff, awkward swimming.

Potential Causes

- **Stress:** Poor water quality, temperature changes, or overcrowding can cause koi to clamp their fins as a stress response.

- **Parasitic Infections:** Parasites like flukes or lice can cause irritation and discomfort, leading koi to clamp their fins.

- **Infections:** Bacterial or fungal infections can cause koi to clamp their fins, especially if the fins are directly affected by the infection.

7.3 Basic First Aid for Koi

When koi show signs of illness or distress, immediate action is crucial to prevent the situation from escalating. Providing first aid to sick or injured koi can significantly increase their chances of recovery. This involves isolating affected fish, treating symptoms, and addressing the underlying cause of the problem.

7.3.1 Isolating Sick Fish

Isolating a sick koi is the first and most critical step in preventing the spread of disease to other fish in the pond. Koi can suffer from contagious illnesses like bacterial infections, parasites, or viruses that can rapidly infect the entire pond population.

Quarantine Tank Setup

- **Size:** Ensure the quarantine tank is large enough to comfortably house the koi. A 100-200-gallon tank is usually sufficient for short-term isolation.

- **Filtration:** Use a properly sized filter to maintain good water quality. A sponge filter or small external filter works well for quarantine tanks.

- **Aeration:** Oxygenation is essential. Use an air pump with an airstone to ensure adequate oxygen levels.

- **Heater:** In colder months, consider using a heater to maintain stable water temperatures, which can aid in the koi's recovery.

- **Cover:** Provide a secure cover for the quarantine tank to prevent the koi from jumping out, especially if they feel stressed.

- **Duration:** Isolate the koi for at least 2-4 weeks to monitor its condition. During this time, closely observe for any changes in behavior, appetite, or physical appearance.

- **Water Parameters:** Ensure the water in the quarantine tank is well-maintained, with frequent water changes and monitoring of pH, ammonia, and nitrate levels.

7.3.2 Salt Baths

Salt baths are one of the most effective and accessible first aid treatments for koi suffering from external parasites or bacterial infections. Salt is a natural disinfectant and helps relieve stress, improve gill function, and eliminate some parasites.

Preparation

- Use non-iodized salt (like aquarium salt or pond salt) to avoid introducing harmful additives.
- Fill a separate container with pond water to minimize the shock caused by different water parameters.

Method

- Add 1-2 tablespoons of salt per gallon of water to the container. Stir until the salt is fully dissolved.
- Gently place the affected koi in the salt solution.
- Allow the koi to soak for 5-10 minutes, depending on the severity of the condition.
- Monitor the koi carefully. If it shows signs of extreme distress (such as erratic swimming or

gasping), remove it from the salt bath immediately.

Aftercare

- Once the salt bath is complete, transfer the koi back to the quarantine tank. Do not return it to the main pond until its condition improves.

- Salt baths can be repeated daily for up to 3-5 days if necessary, but avoid overexposing the koi to salt, as this can cause harm.

7.3.3 Topical Treatments for Wounds and Ulcers

If your koi has visible injuries, such as ulcers, sores, or cuts, immediate treatment is essential to prevent secondary infections. Topical treatments can be applied to disinfect wounds and promote healing.

Materials Needed

- Clean, soft cloth or paper towel.

- Iodine or an antiseptic fish treatment (available at aquarium stores).
- Cotton swabs or a soft brush for applying the treatment.

Method

- Remove the koi from the water using a soft net and place it on a damp towel to keep it moist.
- Gently clean the wound with a soft cloth or paper towel to remove any debris or slime.
- Apply iodine or a fish-safe antiseptic directly to the affected area using a cotton swab or soft brush. Be careful not to apply too much pressure.
- Once treated, return the koi to the quarantine tank. Avoid placing it back in the main pond until the wound has healed sufficiently.
- **Repeat as Needed:** Reapply the topical treatment every few days, ensuring the koi

remains in a clean environment to prevent infection.

7.3.4 Medicated Food

When koi suffer from internal infections or parasites, medicated food can be an effective form of treatment. This method delivers antibiotics or antiparasitic medications directly into the koi's system, promoting faster recovery.

Types of Medicated Food

- **Antibiotic Food:** Used to treat bacterial infections such as ulcers or fin rot.
- **Antiparasitic Food:** Used to eliminate internal parasites such as flukes or intestinal worms.

Usage

- Administer medicated food as directed on the packaging, usually for 5-10 days.

- Feed the medicated food exclusively during this period. Ensure the koi are eating the food, as some sick fish may refuse food.
- If the koi do not eat, try mixing the medicated food with a small amount of garlic extract, which may stimulate their appetite.

Note: Medicated food should only be used when there is a confirmed diagnosis of bacterial or parasitic infection. Overuse of antibiotics can lead to drug resistance.

7.3.5. Water Quality Adjustments

Poor water quality is often the root cause of koi health problems. The accumulation of toxins such as ammonia, nitrites, and nitrates can weaken koi's immune systems, making them more susceptible to disease.

Testing Water Parameters

Use a reliable water test kit to check the following parameters:

- **Ammonia:** Should be at 0 ppm (parts per million).
- **Nitrite:** Should be at 0 ppm.
- **Nitrate:** Should be kept below 40 ppm.
- **pH:** Ideally between 7.0 and 8.5.
- **Temperature:** Keep the water temperature consistent, avoiding sudden fluctuations.

Corrective Actions

- **Water Changes:** If ammonia or nitrite levels are high, perform a 25-50% water change. Be sure to dechlorinate the water before adding it to the pond or quarantine tank.
- **Filtration:** Check that the pond's filtration system is functioning properly. If necessary,

upgrade the filter or add additional filtration media to improve water quality.

- **Aeration:** Increase aeration with air pumps or fountains to boost oxygen levels, especially in warmer water when dissolved oxygen tends to be lower.

CHAPTER EIGHT

BREEDING KOI

8.1 Understanding Koi Breeding Cycles

Breeding koi is a captivating process that closely follows their natural reproductive behaviors, seasonal changes, and environmental conditions. While koi can breed in captivity, their breeding success relies heavily on your understanding of their breeding cycles, water quality, and the ideal conditions for both the adults and their offspring.

8.1.1 Breeding Season: The Ideal Time for Spawning

Koi are seasonal breeders, with spawning usually triggered by rising water temperatures in spring. These temperature fluctuations signal to koi that the conditions are right for reproduction. In the wild, koi breed in response to both warmer temperatures and longer daylight hours.

Optimal Breeding Temperature

- Koi begin spawning when the water temperature reaches 65-75°F (18-24°C).
- Spawning typically occurs in late spring to early summer.
- The exact timing may vary depending on your geographic location, but the combination of warmer water and an increase in daylight is key.

Natural Instinct

- In their natural environment, spring brings more abundant food and favorable conditions for young koi to grow, which is why koi are biologically programmed to spawn during this time.

- The increase in temperature also makes koi more active, triggering hormonal changes that prepare them for reproduction.

Signs of Readiness

- You may notice koi becoming more active as they engage in mating behaviors.

- The males will start chasing the females around the pond as a prelude to spawning.

8.1.2. Sexual Maturity: When Koi Are Ready to Breed

Koi don't breed until they reach sexual maturity, which occurs as they grow older and larger. The age at which koi become sexually mature can vary slightly depending on environmental factors and their overall health.

Age of Maturity

- Koi typically reach sexual maturity between 3-4 years of age.

- Females tend to mature slightly later than males.

Size and Health Matter

- Larger koi tend to be more successful breeders and produce more eggs.

- Healthy fish with a proper diet and optimal pond conditions are more likely to reach sexual maturity at the right age and breed effectively.

Annual Breeding

- Once koi have reached maturity, they can breed annually during each breeding season as long as conditions are favorable.

- Keep in mind that koi breeding can put physical strain on the fish, so monitoring their health post-breeding is crucial.

8.1.3. Identifying Male and Female Koi

Distinguishing between male and female koi is essential when preparing for breeding. While the differences may not be immediately obvious in young or immature fish, sexually mature koi exhibit distinct characteristics.

Female Koi

- Females are generally larger and rounder, particularly in the belly area.

- During the breeding season, females will become even rounder as they carry eggs. Their abdomen will feel soft and swollen to the touch.

- Female koi also tend to have a bulkier and wider body shape, particularly near the middle and rear of their bodies.

Male Koi

- Males are usually slimmer and more streamlined compared to females.

- During breeding season, males develop breeding tubercles—small, white, pimple-like spots on their gill covers and pectoral fins. These tubercles help the males nudge females during the spawning process.

- Males are more likely to display aggressive or persistent chasing behavior during the breeding season as they try to encourage females to release their eggs.

8.1.4. Breeding Behavior: The Process of Spawning

Koi spawning is an active and vigorous process that involves a series of courtship behaviors, egg-laying, and fertilization.

Chasing and Nudging

- The first visible sign of spawning behavior is the males chasing the females around the pond.

- This chasing can be quite intense and may last several hours. Males nudge the females' sides and underbellies to encourage them to release eggs.
- While this behavior is natural, it can be stressful for the female, so it's important to ensure that the pond environment is safe and free of sharp objects or hazards that could injure her.

Egg Laying

- When the female is ready, she will release her eggs into the pond. The eggs are sticky and adhere to pond surfaces like plants, spawning mops, or even rocks.
- Koi are prolific breeders, with a single female laying anywhere from 50,000 to 100,000 eggs depending on her size.

Fertilization

- As soon as the eggs are released, the male koi will fertilize the eggs by releasing milt (sperm) over them.

- This fertilization process happens externally, so the presence of both males and females in the pond is necessary for successful breeding.

Post-Spawning

- After the eggs have been fertilized, the adults' involvement is over. In fact, koi will often try to eat their own eggs if given the opportunity, so it's crucial to protect the eggs by removing the adults or placing spawning media in the pond for egg collection.

- It's also a good idea to provide adequate plant cover or spawning mats where the eggs can safely adhere.

8.1.5. Caring for the Eggs and Fry

Once the eggs have been fertilized, they will hatch within 4-7 days, depending on the water temperature. Warmer water speeds up the hatching process, while cooler water slows it down.

Protecting the Eggs

Since koi are known to consume their eggs, it's often recommended to either:

- Remove the adults from the breeding pond immediately after spawning, or
- Use spawning nets or mats to collect the eggs and move them to a separate hatching tank.

Egg Incubation

- Maintain water quality by using gentle filtration and aeration to ensure oxygen levels remain high.
- Water temperature should be kept within the 65-75°F (18-24°C) range to promote healthy hatching.

Hatching and Early Fry Care

- Once the eggs hatch, the koi fry is extremely small and delicate. For the first few days, they will feed on their egg yolk sacs.

- After this, they will begin feeding on microscopic organisms in the water, so it's important to ensure the pond or hatching tank has plenty of infusoria (small aquatic organisms that fry can eat).

- You can supplement their diet with specially formulated fry food, such as finely ground flakes or live food like baby brine shrimp.

8.2 Preparing Your Pond for Spawning

Creating an ideal environment for koi spawning is essential to ensure the health and safety of both the adult koi and their eggs. Proper preparation of the pond helps promote natural breeding behaviors while reducing risks such as injuries, stress, and egg predation. Here's a detailed guide on how to prepare your pond for successful koi spawning.

8.2.1. Pond Size and Space: Providing Ample Room for Spawning

The size of your pond plays a significant role in ensuring successful spawning. During the breeding season, koi become very active, particularly the males who chase the females as part of their courtship ritual. A small or overcrowded pond can lead to stress and physical injury during these aggressive interactions.

Adequate Space

- Ensure that your pond is large enough to comfortably accommodate all your koi. For breeding purposes, a minimum pond size of 1,000 gallons is recommended, although larger ponds (around 3,000 gallons or more) are ideal.

- Koi can reach lengths of 18-36 inches when fully grown, so providing ample space ensures that the fish can swim and breed without feeling cramped.

Avoid Overcrowding

- Overcrowding can lead to territorial aggression during breeding and make it difficult for the koi to complete the spawning process.
- To prevent overcrowding, consider reducing the number of fish in the pond by moving some to a separate pond or quarantine tank during the breeding season.

8.2.2. Spawning Mats: Creating Safe Spaces for Eggs

In the wild, koi would lay their eggs on submerged plants and other structures. In a controlled pond environment, it's essential to provide surfaces where the eggs can safely attach and develop. Spawning mats are a popular and effective solution for this purpose.

Choosing Spawning Materials

- **Spawning Mats:** These are made from soft, fibrous material that mimics the natural environment where koi would lay their eggs. They provide an ideal surface for the sticky eggs to adhere to.

- **Alternative Options:** You can also use water hyacinth roots, breeding brushes, or even submerged aquatic plants like anacharis or hornwort as alternatives to spawning mats. These materials replicate the textures koi seek when laying eggs.

Placement of Spawning Mats

- Place the spawning mats in shallow areas or around the edges of the pond, as koi tend to prefer these spots for laying their eggs.

- Ensure the mats are positioned securely so they don't move around during the active breeding process.

- Multiple mats should be used in various locations to increase the chances of egg attachment and to reduce competition for space.

Density of Coverage

Providing enough coverage is crucial. Make sure that the mats or plants cover at least 20-30% of the pond's shallow areas, giving the female koi plenty of places to deposit her eggs.

8.2.3. Protecting the Eggs: Preventing Egg Predation

Once the female koi releases her eggs, both the male and female may eat them if left unprotected. To ensure the survival of the eggs, specific measures must be taken to shield them from predation.

Removing Spawning Mats

- **Egg Transfer:** One of the most effective methods of egg protection is to remove the spawning mats from the main pond immediately after spawning.

The mats can be transferred to a separate tank or pond dedicated to hatching the eggs.

- The separate hatching area should have optimal water quality, filtration, and aeration, with a stable water temperature of 65-75°F (18-24°C) to promote egg development and hatching.

Keeping Mats in the Pond

- If you prefer not to move the mats, ensure that the eggs have adequate hiding spots. Adding dense aquatic plants or shelters can help conceal the eggs from hungry adults.

- You may also consider adding egg guards or placing mesh nets over the spawning mats to prevent adult koi from reaching the eggs while still allowing oxygen flow and water circulation.

8.2.4. Water Quality: Maintaining Optimal Conditions

Water quality is crucial during the breeding season, as poor conditions can negatively affect the adults and the developing eggs. Stable, clean water promotes healthier spawning behavior and reduces the risk of infections, parasites, or egg mortality.

Filtration System

- Ensure your pond's filtration system is functioning optimally to maintain clear water. It should be able to handle the increased biological load caused by the breeding activity.

- Perform regular maintenance on filters and remove any debris or algae buildup that could compromise water quality.

Monitoring Water Parameters

- Conduct water tests regularly to check key parameters such as pH, ammonia, nitrite, and nitrate levels. High levels of ammonia or nitrites can be toxic to both adults and eggs, while an imbalance in pH can cause stress to breeding koi.

- Maintain a pH between 7.0-8.0 and ensure ammonia and nitrite levels are at 0 ppm. Nitrates should be kept under 40 ppm.

Water Changes

Regular partial water changes can help keep the water clean and oxygenated. Change around 10-20% of the water every week to reduce waste buildup and maintain stable water chemistry.

Aeration

Ensure adequate aeration in the pond, especially in warmer months when oxygen levels naturally decrease. Use air stones or waterfalls to increase oxygenation, which benefits both adult koi and developing eggs.

8.2.5. Reducing Stress: Creating a Peaceful Environment

Spawning is a demanding process for koi, so it's vital to minimize stress during the breeding season. Stress can weaken the koi's immune system, making them more susceptible to infections, and it can also lead to unsuccessful spawning.

Avoid Handling

Refrain from handling or moving the koi during the breeding season unless absolutely necessary. Handling can cause stress and injury, which can hinder the spawning process.

Limit Disruptions

Keep the pond environment as peaceful as possible. Avoid loud noises or sudden changes in water flow or temperature. Providing a calm environment allows the koi to focus on breeding and reduces stress-related complications.

Monitor for Injuries

The vigorous chasing and nudging that occurs during spawning can sometimes result in minor injuries to the female koi. Watch for signs of physical damage, such as torn fins or scrapes, and be ready to provide first aid (e.g., salt baths or topical treatments) if needed.

8.3 Raising Koi Fry: Care and Feeding

Raising koi fry from hatching to maturity requires careful attention to their environment, feeding habits, and growth stages. Newly hatched fry are particularly vulnerable, and their care needs to be meticulously managed to ensure their survival and healthy development. Here's a detailed guide on caring for koi fry:

8.3.1. Egg Incubation: Monitoring and Protecting the Eggs

After koi spawn, the eggs require a controlled environment for incubation. Proper care during this period is crucial to prevent egg loss due to poor water conditions, fungal infections, or predators.

Hatching Time

- Koi eggs typically hatch within 4-7 days, depending on water temperature. Warmer temperatures around 70-75°F (21-24°C) encourage faster hatching, while cooler water may slow the process.

- Constant oxygenation is essential during this phase. Make sure your filtration system or aeration devices (such as air stones) are working efficiently to keep the water well-oxygenated.

Preventing Fungal Growth

- Fungus is a common threat to koi eggs. Fungal infections usually appear as white, fuzzy growths on the eggs and can spread rapidly, killing healthy eggs in the process.

- Check the eggs daily and remove any infected eggs immediately to prevent the fungus from spreading.

- Consider using an anti-fungal treatment such as methylene blue or commercially available anti-fungal products. Ensure these treatments are safe for koi fry and use only as directed.

8.3.2. Fry Hatch and First Days: Ensuring a Safe Start

When koi fry first hatch, they are incredibly delicate and highly vulnerable. During this time, it's essential to provide a safe and nurturing environment.

Yolk Sac Nutrition

Newly hatched fry have a yolk sac attached to their bodies, which provides them with all the necessary nutrients for the first 3-5 days. During this time, they will remain mostly stationary, absorbing nourishment from the yolk.

Avoid feeding them during this period, as they are not yet ready for external food.

Predator-Free Environment

Protect the fry from predators, including adult koi or other pond inhabitants, by keeping them in a separate tank or pond. Using a dedicated fry tank helps reduce the risk of predation and allows you to maintain better control over water conditions.

Aeration and Water Quality

- Ensure the fry tank is equipped with proper aeration to keep the water oxygenated. Fry are particularly sensitive to low oxygen levels, which can lead to high mortality rates.

- Maintain excellent water quality from the moment the fry hatch. Even small fluctuations in water parameters like ammonia or nitrite can be fatal to newly hatched koi fry.

8.3.3. Fry Feeding: Nutritional Needs in Early Development

Feeding koi fry correctly is essential for their growth and survival. They need tiny, nutrient-dense food sources to support their rapid development.

First Food

- Once the yolk sac is absorbed, fry will begin swimming and are ready for external food. Initially, fry should be fed microscopic food such as:

- Infusoria (tiny aquatic organisms, ideal for young fry).

- **Liquid fry food:** Specialized commercial food that is designed for fish fry.

- **Finely powdered fry food:** Commercial foods that are ground to a fine powder for easy digestion.

Gradual Transition to Larger Foods

- As the fry grow, they will need larger food items. Gradually introduce them to foods such as:

- **Baby brine shrimp:** A highly nutritious food source that is easy for fry to digest.

- **Daphnia:** Small aquatic crustaceans that provide protein and promote growth.

- **Finely crushed koi pellets:** As the fry develop, finely crushing regular koi pellets can provide them with the essential nutrients needed for healthy growth.

Feeding Frequency

- Fry grow rapidly and have fast metabolisms, so they need to be fed multiple times a day—typically 3-4 times. Frequent, small feedings ensure that the fry have access to enough nutrition without fouling the water.

8.3.4. Water Quality: The Key to Healthy Fry

Maintaining optimal water quality is paramount when raising koi fry. Poor water conditions can stunt growth, cause disease, or even kill fry.

Frequent Water Changes

Fry are highly sensitive to ammonia and nitrite buildup, so small, frequent water changes are necessary. Change 10-20% of the water every 2-3 days to keep toxins in check while avoiding abrupt changes in water chemistry.

Monitor Water Parameters

- Test the water regularly for ammonia, nitrite, nitrate, and pH levels. Keep ammonia and nitrite levels at 0 ppm, while nitrates should remain below 20-40 ppm. Maintain a pH range of 7.0-8.0 for optimal fry development.

- Keep the water temperature stable between 70-75°F (21-24°C). Sudden temperature fluctuations can stress the fry and lead to high mortality.

Filtration and Aeration

- Use a gentle filtration system that won't harm the delicate fry. A sponge filter is ideal for fry tanks as it provides mechanical and biological filtration without creating strong currents that could overwhelm young fry.

- Ensure proper aeration to keep oxygen levels high. Fry have higher oxygen needs than adult koi, so maintaining dissolved oxygen levels is essential for their survival and growth.

8.3.5. Growth Stages: From Fry to Juveniles

Koi fry go through various growth stages, and each stage has specific care requirements. Monitoring their development and adjusting their environment and food accordingly is key to raising healthy juveniles.

1-2 Inches in Length

- By the time the fry reach about 1-2 inches in length, they will start exhibiting stronger swimming behaviors and increased food competition. At this stage, it's essential to separate larger fry from smaller ones to ensure everyone gets enough food.

- Larger fry can outcompete smaller ones, leading to starvation for the smaller fish. Use a grow-out tank for larger fry, allowing them to continue developing without overshadowing smaller individuals.

Coloration and Pattern Development

- Around 6-8 weeks of age, the fry will begin developing their distinctive koi colors and patterns. Initially, most fry will appear pale or grey, but as they mature, their colors will start to show.

- Koi coloration will continue to evolve over the next several months. Be patient when selecting which fry to keep, as the final colors and patterns may not be apparent until they are several months old.

Selective Culling

- In large batches of koi fry, culling (removing weaker or undesirable fry) may be necessary to manage the population. Culling helps ensure that the healthiest and best-colored fry get enough food and space to thrive.

8.3.6. Predator Control: Keeping the Fry Safe

Fry are especially vulnerable to predators, so it's important to take extra measures to protect them.

Separate Fry Tank

If possible, keep the fry in a separate tank or pond until they are large enough to survive alongside adult koi and other pond inhabitants.

Predator Deterrents

If raising fry in an outdoor pond, consider adding protective netting over the pond to keep out birds and other predators that might target the small fry.

CONCLUSION

As you complete your journey through this comprehensive guide to koi fish care, you've now gained the knowledge and confidence to create a thriving and beautiful koi pond. Koi fish, with their vibrant colors and graceful movements, are more than just ornamental fish; they are living works of art that bring peace, serenity, and joy to any environment. Caring for koi is a rewarding experience that requires dedication, patience, and attention to detail. From designing the perfect pond, maintaining water quality, and feeding your koi, to understanding their health needs and even breeding your own koi, each step is a crucial part of ensuring your fish lead long, healthy lives. As you continue on your koi-keeping adventure, remember that success comes from observing your fish, learning from your experiences, and staying committed to their well-being. Whether you're a beginner or an experienced hobbyist, the joy of watching your koi grow and thrive is an experience that deepens your connection to these magnificent creatures.

Made in United States
Orlando, FL
13 December 2024